The Real Race Revolutionaries

How Minority Entrepreneurship Can Overcome America's Racial and Economic Divides

The Real Race Revolutionaries

How Minority Entrepreneurship Can Overcome America's Racial and Economic Divides

ALFREDO ORTIZ

Foreword by Bernie Marcus

DEFIANCE PRESS & PUBLISHING

The Real Race Revolutionaries: How Minority Entrepreneurship Can Overcome America's Racial and Economic Divides

This book is a work of non-fiction. The author has made every effort to ensure that the accuracy of the information in this book was correct at the time of the publication. Neither the author nor the publisher nor any other person(s) associated with this book may be held liable for any damages that may result from any of the ideas made by the author in this book.

ISBN-13: 978-1-959677-06-2 (Paperback)
ISBN-13: 978-1-959677-05-5 (eBook)

Published by Defiance Press & Publishing, LLC

Bulk orders of this book may be obtained by contacting Defiance Press & Publishing, LLC. www.defiancepress.com.

Public Relations Dept. – Defiance Press & Publishing, LLC
281-581-9300
pr@defiancepress.com

Defiance Press & Publishing, LLC
281-581-9300
info@defiancepress.com

The author would like to thank Jordan Bruneau for his help with this book.

To my mother, Gloria, who taught me to never back away from a challenge just because it seems huge but rather to push into it, head-on, and never give up.

TABLE OF CONTENTS

FOREWORD: ENSURING THE NEXT GENERATION OF HOME DEPOTS

N o one has experienced entrepreneurship's ability to help minorities improve their economic circumstances more than me—and that's not only because I'm ninety-three years old.

I saw the power of entrepreneurship firsthand after co-founding The Home Depot, a company that revolutionized the home improvement industry and empowered millions of disproportionately minority Americans to realize their entrepreneurial dreams. My experiences have led me to believe preserving and expanding entrepreneurship is the key to advancing America's racial and economic equality.

I was born to Jewish immigrant parents and grew up poor in tenement housing in Newark. I dreamed of becoming a doctor and eventually got accepted into Harvard Medical School. This feat was especially impressive given the widespread anti-Semitism and quota system medical schools used to deny Jewish applicants at the time. But despite this accomplishment, my family couldn't afford the tuition.

Minorities today encounter similar hurdles to succeeding in competitive industries such as medicine, law, and finance. Asians continue to face *de facto* quotas at American universities. Black and brown Americans often have fewer resources and connections. Many minorities come from bad neighborhoods, broken families, and terrible public schools.

Entrepreneurship offers all Americans—no matter their background—a side door to achieving financial independence and the American Dream. It's still difficult for a minority high school graduate from Newark to excel in corporate America—but entrepreneurship gives them another path. Entrepreneurship rewards goods and services that the market values, independent of the SAT scores, financial resources, or personal pedigrees of the people selling them.

I ended up in the home improvement industry. I worked my way up the corporate ladder only to be fired by a capricious boss. Afterward, I was unemployed at forty-nine. I had every reason to be bitter. But I turned to entrepreneurship, which made my life's second act far better than I ever could have imagined.

With almost no money, I had the idea to start a hardware store, a lumberyard, and a garden store all in one. What began as a single store in Georgia grew to over two thousand locations nationwide and made me a billionaire in the process. Only in America could an ethnic minority from a poor immigrant family have a success story like mine.

The financial rewards pale in comparison to the emotional rewards of seeing how The Home Depot has helped countless others become financially independent through entrepreneurship. The Home Depot democratized the home improvement, landscaping, and building trades so that anyone willing to work up a sweat and learn some basic skills could immediately start a sole proprietorship or small business servicing the nation's eighty million homeowners.

You can observe the entrepreneurs that The Home Depot helped spawn driving around town in their well-loved trucks full of tools and material. Many of these entrepreneurs are minorities. They don't consider themselves victims of racial wealth or income gaps; in fact, they are actively overcoming racial economic disparities through their work.

This phenomenon isn't only occurring in the building and landscaping professions. In almost every part of the economy, you'll find entrepreneurial minorities breaking through difficult circumstances to achieve and live the American Dream. Accelerating this process is the key to closing racial economic divides still plaguing the nation.

Unfortunately, the nation is moving in the wrong direction, erecting numerous hurdles to entrepreneurship. The Home Depot wouldn't have succeeded if it had started in today's climate of big government regulations and taxes that disproportionately burden small businesses. The Home Depot almost went bankrupt several times in its first decade, and today's policy environment would have tipped us into insolvency—as it does to countless entrepreneurs each year.

The biggest victims of bad government policy aren't the elite; they will always be able to get into good schools and get their foot in the door of corporate America. The people hurt most by big government are minorities, those who often already face disadvantages in becoming economically independent.

President Ronald Reagan said, "Freedom is never more than one generation away from extinction. We didn't pass it to our children in the bloodstream. It must be fought for, protected, and handed on for them to do the same."

In 2013, I founded the Job Creators Network to fight for freedom and educate the public about how taxes, regulations, and reckless spending negatively impact American entrepreneurship and broader societal well-being.

Alfredo Ortiz has done an excellent job leading the Job Creators

Network in this battle. With him at the helm, JCN has defended small businesses from bad government policies and ushered in free-market reforms that make starting and growing small businesses easier. In this book, he persuasively makes the case that the government must do less, not more, to allow minority entrepreneurs to achieve the American Dream and overcome racial economic disparities.

Celebrating the stories and successes of minority entrepreneurs can generate the public support needed to defend the free-market economy against big government threats. These ordinary entrepreneurs are the heroes of modern-day America, even if they are frequently treated as villains by government officials who siphon their resources to fund their latest social policy aims.

This book asks you to treat minority entrepreneurs with the respect they deserve, and to consider how bad public policy prevents them from surviving and thriving. A newfound respect for minority entrepreneurs, who have done so much with so little, can provide the societal foundation needed to ensure the next generation of Home Depots. It can lay the groundwork for even more minority entrepreneurship success stories than I've seen in my lifetime.

Entrepreneurship is freedom. There is no dichotomy between the two. By defending the former, we can preserve the latter for generations to come.

Bernie Marcus
Co-Founder and Former CEO, The Home Depot
Founder, Job Creators Network
Atlanta, January 2023

INTRODUCTION: THE BUSINESS OF AMERICA IS SMALL BUSINESS

I was recently in an Atlanta bookstore and came across a title marketed to grade-schoolers called *Sylvia and Marsha Start a Revolution.* The book's cover depicts two women of color. According to its Amazon description, the book is "a playful introduction to trans identities," telling the story of "the transgender women of color who fought for LGBTQ+ equality." The moral of this story and so many others like it: kids, especially minority kids, should pursue social activism and "revolution" to make the world a better place.

My thought was: Why can't this book be *Sylvia and Marsha Start a BUSINESS* and feature a tale of entrepreneurship? Starting a business is the real revolutionary act that minorities can take to empower themselves and their communities. Entrepreneurship can bring financial independence and hard-earned confidence. In fact, minority entrepreneurship is a far better vehicle to overcome racial and economic divides than activism.

Want to start a real revolution that actually improves people's lives? Start a business. While it doesn't make newspaper front pages, minorities across the country are doing just this—starting businesses at historic rates and eliminating racial and economic divides through entrepreneurship. This is the message that we should be sending our kids.

A CONFLICT OF VISIONS: ACTIVISM VERSUS ENTREPRENEURSHIP

The debate about the better way to achieve racial economic equality—via activism or entrepreneurship—isn't new. The black intellectuals W.E.B. Du Bois and Booker T. Washington clashed over this question while advocating for racial equality at the turn of the twentieth century. Du Bois argued that activism and political power were the best way for black Americans to attain racial equality, while Washington contended that entrepreneurship was the better approach.

Du Bois believed capitalism to be inherently racist and became a member of the Socialist Party of the United States. He argued that black schools should teach the liberal arts to develop an elite black leadership class. He also called on black Americans to increase their protests and political influence.

Washington, by contrast, believed black Americans should harness the power of capitalism to become economically independent. He called on them to pursue "industry, thrift, education, and property" to attain financial security that would usher in social equality. Of Washington, the historian C. Vann Woodward wrote, "The businessman's gospel of free enterprise, competition, and laissez-faire never had a more loyal exponent." Washington pushed for black schools to focus on trades and entrepreneurship to teach students the skills they needed to earn a living.

Intellectuals and the media have celebrated Du Bois's political approach while Washington has been accused of selling out black interests. Today, Du Bois's spiritual descendants, including black intellectuals Ta-Nehisi Coates and Ibram X. Kendi, are similarly feted for their political activism. ⨯

Yet with time, Washington's entrepreneurial approach has proven the better way to overcome racial and economic divides. Black political dominance in major American cities in recent generations has not translated to racial economic equality. In fact, minority residents in these areas often face high crime and a dearth of economic opportunity. By many economic measures, Barack Obama's presidency was detrimental to black Americans. His anti-capitalist policies reduced entrepreneurship avenues for the most vulnerable Americans.

In contrast, black Americans and other minorities are quietly overcoming racial economic disparities by heeding Washington's call to entrepreneurship. These are the forgotten minorities of America's racial story. Their incredible economic achievements are largely overlooked by society today. These real race revolutionaries eschew media glory for actual racial progress.

These minority entrepreneurs follow in the footsteps of Madam C.J. Walker, a black entrepreneur who became the country's first self-made female millionaire in the early twentieth century. Born immediately after the Emancipation Proclamation—the first in her family not born into a life of slavery—Walker went from a poor plantation worker to a successful business owner in her lifetime.

Like many minority entrepreneurs today, Walker capitalized on a gap in the market. Since most Americans at the time did not have indoor plumbing, they often developed scalp infections. To remedy this problem, Walker developed a haircare system that proved immensely popular with her customers. She leveraged the power of advertising, demonstration, distribution, and multilevel marketing to grow her company nationwide.

"I am a woman who came from the cotton fields of the South," recalled Walker. "From there, I was promoted to the washtub. From there, I was promoted to the cook kitchen. And from there, I promoted myself into the business of manufacturing hair goods and preparations. I have built my own factory on my own ground."

Beyond developing a successful cosmetics business that catered to black American haircare, Walker also empowered tens of thousands of black associates who traveled door-to-door selling her products and earning high commissions. She worked incredibly hard to succeed and overcome her difficult starting circumstances. "When I was a washer-woman, I was an excellent washerwoman," said Walker. "I always took pride in my work and knew that hard work was important." Today's growing population of successful minority entrepreneurs overcoming racial economic disparities serve as the spiritual descendants of Madam C.J. Walker and Booker T. Washington.

MINORITY ENTREPRENEURSHIP IS INCREASINGLY THE BUSINESS OF AMERICA

President Calvin Coolidge said, "The chief business of the American people is business." I'd edit this statement to say the business of America is *small* business, and increasingly minority small business.

The United States is home to thirty-two million small businesses, including six million with employees. Small businesses drive employment, innovation, and economic growth. Two-thirds of new jobs are created by small businesses.

Small businesses are modern-day alchemists: They create value where it didn't exist before. They turn water into wine. Their economic impact reverberates throughout their communities and supplier networks.

Americans' living standards and well-being are directly correlated to the health of small businesses. That's precisely why I've dedicated my professional life to fighting for entrepreneurs as the president and

CEO of the nation's leading small business advocacy organization, the Job Creators Network. We are protecting the backbone of the economic powerhouse that is the United States of America.

American small businesses were dealt an enormous blow by the Covid-19 pandemic and ensuing government restrictions on business activity. Millions of companies across the country were forced to close, many never to return. Small businesses that survived the challenges of Covid-19 now face numerous economic headwinds, including historic inflation, stagflation, recession, and the constant threat of new regulations and taxes. There's never been a more critical time to fight for small businesses.

Fighting for small businesses means fighting for racial minorities. Over my career as a businessman and advocate, I've seen firsthand how minorities are capitalizing on entrepreneurship opportunities to ascend from difficult starting circumstances and enter the middle class. Entrepreneurship can therefore also improve racial income equality.

Minorities are disproportionately entrepreneurial, starting businesses far more often than their white counterparts. Though you won't read it in the mainstream media or hear about it from progressive politicians who practice identity politics, minority entrepreneurs tend to have average incomes and wealth that exceed those of white Americans. This book therefore makes the case that promoting minority entrepreneurship is the most effective way to overcome racial economic disparities.

THE BEST WAY FOR THE GOVERNMENT TO HELP CLOSE RACIAL ECONOMIC DIVIDES IS TO DO LESS

Ironically, big government policy proposals, often made in the name of helping disadvantaged minorities, threaten to block this pathway to racial income equality. Progressives routinely claim that our economic system, which has generated the most vibrant minority middle class in history, is systemically racist and in need of structural reform. In reality, it's their own policies that make it harder for minorities to succeed.

Consider which business has a more difficult time contending with a $15 minimum wage: the neighborhood dry cleaner, or the downtown law firm? Who is more impacted by inflation caused by deficit spending and easy monetary policy: the owner of a local barbecue joint, or the CEO of a financial services company? Which entrepreneur is more affected by runaway gas prices caused by progressives' opposition to traditional energy: the landscaping business that operates out of a 2005 Toyota Tacoma, or an internet entrepreneur who works from his home laptop? And so on—you get the idea.

The book argues that the best way to accelerate minority entrepreneurship and overcome racial economic gaps is for the government to do less, not more.

Progressives claim the moral high ground on racial issues, assuming their policies help overcome racial divides, but the free-market small business economy is actually helping minorities reduce racial income equality through their own volition. In fact, the best antidote to the remaining vestiges of racism is the free-market system that rewards entrepreneurs of all backgrounds based on merit, not identity. Small businesses and their defenders are the ones who genuinely deserve moral authority on race issues.

This book grew from the congressional testimony I offered before the US House of Representatives Ways and Means Committee in the spring of 2022 in a hearing on the barriers facing minority-owned small businesses. I explained how bad government policy—not racism—is the biggest barrier to minority economic opportunity. I pointed to real-world stories of minority small businesses struggling to contend with government burdens.

My perspective was met with backlash from congressional Democrats who tried to steer the discussion to proposed "solutions" involving new racial equity government programs and regulations. One congressman even implied my argument—based on a decade of defending countless small businesses nationwide—was "ignorant."

As the saying goes, when all you have is a hammer, everything looks like a nail. And when you're a progressive politician, every societal issue, including racial economic inequality, must have a big-government response.

I KNOW THE POWER OF MINORITY ENTREPRENEURSHIP FIRSTHAND

This book includes many stories of successful minority immigrants who overcame significant challenges to improve their economic situations—a group I'm fortunate to be a part of.

My parents came to the United States over fifty years ago from Mexico City to pursue the American Dream. My dad was a tailor; my mom, a housekeeper. They struggled at times throughout my childhood. I remember Mom bringing us to St. Rose Church of Lima in Chula Vista, California, to distribute USDA milk and cheese to needy families. After a day's work, we brought our share home too. Every time, we went home last.

They've both passed on, but the values my parents instilled in me—hard work, grit, and gratitude—helped me become a successful small business owner. I've lived the challenges and opportunities facing minority entrepreneurs firsthand. Millions of minority entrepreneurs from Asia, Africa, South America, and the Middle East come here for the same reasons my parents did: to take advantage of America's free-market economy, which rewards ingenuity, hard work, and customer service over credentials, family connections, and skin color.

America's vibrant opportunity economy allowed me to succeed at the highest levels of business. Prior to leading JCN, I was vice president of sales at CSM Bakery, a company that supplies baked goods to major retailers nationwide, and a business consultant at Boston Consulting Group. I later founded my own business strategy and development company called Grupo MAS, which the Zyman Group subsequently acquired. I have also held executive positions at Georgia-Pacific and Kraft Foods, where I was responsible for product innovation.

These experiences have enabled me to better understand the daily challenges facing small businesses. I saw up close how small businesses are at a competitive disadvantage because they lack the economies of scale, preferential purchasing agreements, and profit margins of their big-business counterparts. As a result, bad government policy naturally impacts small businesses to a far greater degree. That's especially true for minority entrepreneurs, whose companies tend to be less profitable and more precarious.

Having witnessed the countless minority small business success stories over the years, I firmly believe that expanding entrepreneurship opportunities is the best way to close America's racial economic gaps.

THE CASE FOR MINORITY ENTREPRENEURSHIP

In the following six chapters, I'll make the case for minority entrepreneurship and call on the government to, simply put, get out of the way.

Chapter 1 draws on anecdotal and empirical research to discuss how minorities are already overcoming racial economic disparities through entrepreneurship. I show how entrepreneurship is also helping minorities indirectly by providing job opportunities and skills that lift up communities and generate higher financial returns.

Chapter 2 challenges the progressive argument that racial economic differences are a product of racism. I argue that the free market, which is truly anti-racist, is the best way to eliminate racism that remains in our country.

Chapter 3 explains America's minority entrepreneurship advantage, highlighting how minorities have voted with their feet by coming to the United States over other developed countries to pursue their dreams. I point to high pay rates, low taxes, free labor markets, and an established culture of entrepreneurship to explain America's minority entrepreneurship outperformance.

Chapter 4 addresses the biggest threats facing minority entrepreneurs, namely well-intended government policies that have only made it more difficult for them to achieve the American Dream. Progressive policy solutions such as tax increases, new labor and environment regulations, and new social programs would kill these small-business golden geese and exacerbate racial economic inequality.

Chapter 5 offers public policy solutions to accelerate minority entrepreneurship. These include making small business tax cuts permanent, ending inflationary deficit spending, recommitting to traditional energy sources, and eliminating pointless regulations. In stark contrast to progressives, I argue the government is the problem, not the solution to racial economic equality.

Chapter 6 concludes with the choice facing this country: Will we move toward socialism or capitalism? Will we remember the forgotten men and women who run small businesses, or treat them as a means to progressives' social ends? The answers to such questions will determine whether America's small-business economy survives intact, and whether we can continue progressing toward real racial economic equality.

If the United States chooses to sacrifice its remarkable economic opportunity in the name of racial progress, it will get neither. However, if we recommit to defending the free-market small business economy, we will get both. Minorities can close today's racial economic gaps through entrepreneurship—but to be able to do so, the business of America must remain small business.

CHAPTER 1: MINORITY ENTREPRENEURSHIP CAN OVERCOME RACIAL ECONOMIC GAPS

Carlton Guthrie and his brother are the owners of Detroit Chassis, a business that assembles chassis for Ford motorhomes and commercial trucks. In fact, it supplies chassis to all the nation's big RV companies and offers custom chassis modifications. In recent years, the business opened a new plant in Ohio to assemble rear axles, tires, and wheels for Ford's medium-duty trucks.

Carlton grew the company from a small metal-stamping unit into one of the biggest black-owned manufacturers in Michigan. At present it earns over $100 million a year in revenue from Ford alone and employs roughly 160 workers, most of whom are black. Like all of the country's most successful entrepreneurs, Carlton identified opportunities to horizontally and vertically integrate his business, growing it to the point where it can produce all complex automotive components.

"Ford was looking for better ideas, and we had several," Carlton told me. His company was able to do what many political commentators have thought was impossible: return automotive manufacturing from Mexico back home to Michigan. In 1999, he convinced Ford to contract through his company by offering the entrepreneur's trifecta of higher quality, faster turnaround, and better value. His sophisticated assembly plant has saved Ford millions of dollars on production and shipping for its motor homes. "Ford really appreciated that we were willing to operate in a partnership mode," he notes.

Born in Gary, Indiana, to humble beginnings, Carlton has lived the American Dream and overcome racial disparities through entrepreneurship. His entrepreneurial efforts have earned him significant accolades, including Michigan Manufacturer of the Year and Chivas Regal Entrepreneur of the Year.

The financial rewards that Carlton has earned from his entrepreneurial activity, however, pale in comparison to what he has given back to his community. Over the decades, Carlton has created thousands of quality jobs for black workers in some of the most economically distressed parts of the state.

"It's part of our mission statement to create programs that impact the communities in which we exist," he tells me. "We've always looked at our employees as integral members of not just our business but our community and find ways to help support them. The more you do for them, the more they do for you."

Like many minority business owners, Carlton has provided employment lifelines for his community. "We hire people most folks wouldn't," he states, including ex-convicts from the nearby Jackson State Prison.

"The first folks we hired were women from a welfare-to-work program, many of whom had never worked in manufacturing," he recalls. "We provided them with support services, and these women turned out to be fantastic employees. Some of them went on to management, making six figures." Others earned $25 an hour or more as employees at Detroit Chassis, or they took the skills they had learned to earn a similar pay with other manufacturers in the area. Many of these women were single mothers.

"Our goal is to reach out and provide not just jobs but services," he explains. "We even have a company chaplain to help people with spiritual guidance and direction."

"Minority businesses typically share a much larger load in terms of their contribution to their communities," he says. "We can't match the size of big businesses, but we are 'outsized' members of our communities. Most black businesses are embedded in their communities, providing jobs, products, economic activity, and services."

After a lifetime of highly successful and arduous entrepreneurial work, Carlton is turning his focus to helping the next generation of black entrepreneurs. He travels to schools in Detroit, Chicago, and Gary to inspire kids with a message of community responsibility, business success, and financial freedom. He frames his lessons around what he calls the "Four *G*'s": God, goals, guidance, and guts.

His main advice: focus on developing real skills. "It's great if you've got an idea, but it takes a myriad of skills to bring those ideas to bear." Skill-building will empower almost anyone to succeed in today's entrepreneurial economy, regardless of their background.

"There's a [special] connection black businesses have with their employees and communities," says Carlton. "It's clear that black businesses are integral to and integrated into their communities."

MINORITY ENTREPRENEURSHIP CAN OVERCOME RACIAL ECONOMIC GAPS

Like all entrepreneurs, Carlton is a modern-day alchemist, creating value where it didn't exist before. These entrepreneurs embody the uniquely American phrase to "make money," with "money" signifying the creation of goods and services that society wants and needs.

They do so by trading value for value in win-win relationships that help their customers, employees, suppliers, and communities. They are the fountainheads of economic growth, higher living standards, and employment opportunities. To put it simply, these entrepreneurs are the heroes of modern-day America.

Minority entrepreneurs like Carlton also represent the best opportunity possible to close racial economic gaps that currently plague our country. Countless minority entrepreneurs all across the United States are quietly taking similar entrepreneurial action to improve their livelihoods and overcome racial economic disparities for themselves and their employees through their own initiative. They embody the entrepreneurial path forward to improve racial economic equality.

For all the country's racial progress (especially compared with other nations), racial income and wealth gaps remain significant. In 2019, the median white household income was $76,057, versus $56,113 for median Hispanic households and $46,073 for median black households. (It is worth noting that incomes were slightly lower among all races in 2020 due to the pandemic.) In other words, white households earn roughly 50 percent more than Hispanic and black households.

An even more significant racial disparity exists when measuring wealth. According to the Federal Reserve's Survey of Consumer Finances, the median net worth of white households in 2019 was $189,000, versus $36,000 for Hispanic households and $24,000 for black households. White households have about eight times the wealth of black households and five times the wealth of Hispanic households.

However, the median Asian household income was $98,174 in 2019—nearly 30 percent greater than the median white household. This Asian outperformance undercuts the progressive claim that racial economic gaps are a product of racism (a topic I'll address in-depth in the next chapter).

Racial economic gaps disrupt American social harmony. Progressives use them to pit races against each other, fostering tribal and collectivist policy responses that violate America's tradition of individual rights and reduce economic opportunities minorities could use to improve racial economic equality.

American ghettos and barrios foster violence, gangs, and intergenerational poverty. They represent trillions of dollars in foregone economic opportunity. Citibank estimates that the racial wealth gap has cost the US economy $16 trillion over the past twenty years.

Entrepreneurship is the key to closing these gaps. Treasury Secretary Janet Yellen has classified business ownership as a key avenue to mitigating wealth inequality. Entrepreneurship, she argues, is "a significant source of economic opportunity for many families below the very top in income and wealth."

"The last great, untapped asset class in America is hiding in plain sight," argues Philip Gaskin, vice president of entrepreneurship at the Kauffman Foundation. Increasing minority entrepreneurship is the "key to unlocking billion to trillions of dollars ... while creating opportunity for millions who don't have it now."

Entrepreneurship gives minorities the opportunity to immediately create value, earn income, and generate wealth to overcome the racial economic disparities they face. Entrepreneurship offers a ticket to the middle class; it provides a path to financial security for people of all backgrounds, regardless of education, class, connections, and experience. With hard work and a knowledge of the marketplace, minorities can overcome racial economic inequalities.

MINORITY ENTREPRENEURS ARE ALREADY OVERCOMING RACIAL ECONOMIC DISPARITIES

A Congressional Black Caucus Foundation study found that the median net worth for black business owners is twelve times higher than for black non-business owners. In other words, black entrepreneurs more than eliminate racial income and wealth gaps, earning and saving far more than median white households.

Research confirms the minority entrepreneurship advantage. In a study published in *Economics Development Quarterly,* University of Washington economist William Bradford explains how entrepreneurship generates higher incomes: "Entrepreneurs bring new and better products to markets, restore allocative efficiency through arbitrage, and reinvest their profits."

Using data from the Panel Study of Income Dynamics, Bradford unsurprisingly discovered that black entrepreneurs have higher upward wealth mobility and wealth levels than black workers. He demonstrates that the black entrepreneurship wealth mobility dividend is equivalent to that of white entrepreneurs. If black entrepreneurs can continue their recent outperformance in wealth mobility, he argues, "then increasing the rate of black entrepreneurship will reduce the wealth disparity between black and white families."

Similarly, a recent study published in the *Journal of Economics, Race, and Policy* by economists at Brandeis University found that successful black entrepreneurs from the middle third of the American wealth distribution have a 60.5 percent chance of entering the top third of wealth holders within four years. In contrast, black wage earners have a 27.5 percent chance. (See chart below.)

In other words, black entrepreneurs have more than twice the opportunity to move to the top tercile of earners compared to their employed counterparts. The study also concluded that black entrepreneurs have a nearly 20 percent greater chance of moving into the top third of wealth earners than white entrepreneurs. The study holds constant between entrepreneurs and workers other variables that may otherwise have impacted wealth mobility, such as education, family, lack of inheritance, and health.

Percent Chance of Entering Top Wealth Tercile from Below Top Wealth Tercile
Black entrepreneurs are twice as likely as comparable black or white workers to ascend to the top third of wealth holders. They are also significantly more likely than white entrepreneurs to ascend to this tercile.

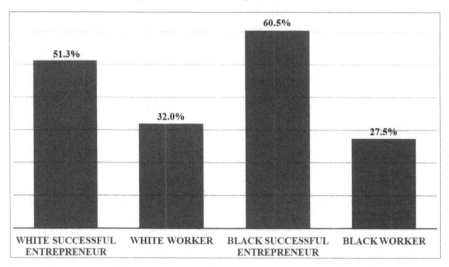

Source: Kroeger and White, *Journal of Economics, Race, and Policy,* 2021

Critics may claim these entrepreneurship benefits suffer from survivorship bias, ignoring the experiences of failed entrepreneurs and cherry-picking the victors. Yet even while broadening the analysis to include unsuccessful black entrepreneurs, the Brandeis study still found that 39.3 percent of all black entrepreneurs entered the top wealth tercile—significantly more than comparable black workers.

Meanwhile, Hispanic entrepreneurship is already helping to close the racial wealth gap. The ratio between white and Hispanic household wealth declined from 8:1 in 2013 to 5:1 in 2019 as Hispanic entrepreneurship skyrocketed.

The median net worth of self-employed Hispanics is $174,920, and the median net worth of self-employed Hispanics with business equity is $314,280. In other words, like their black counterparts, Hispanic entrepreneurs have already succeeded in closing income and wealth gaps with median white Americans. Far from being intractable, as progressives claim, racial economic disparities can and are, in fact, being closed through entrepreneurship.

Even unsuccessful entrepreneurs earn the work experience, skills, and confidence necessary to succeed and draw a higher salary in the job market. Hiring managers are generally impressed by candidates that started their own businesses, even if these enterprises ultimately weren't successful. Employers associate entrepreneurial experience with leadership, responsibility, and self-motivation, all of which are viewed as positive signals that can help minority workers overcome a lack of credentials in the job market.

Minority entrepreneurship also pays racial dividends beyond profits earned by owners. As demonstrated by Carlton's story, minority-owned businesses are often located in minority neighborhoods and hire minorities to work for them. Research suggests that minority businesses are three times as likely to hire minorities as their white counterparts. These job opportunities often provide an employment lifeline for minorities who otherwise wouldn't have options to earn a living, thus helping to further close racial economic gaps.

MINORITIES ARE DISPROPORTIONATELY ENTREPRENEURIAL

Largely because of these outsized returns offered by entrepreneurship, minorities are disproportionately entrepreneurial, starting businesses at a faster rate than white Americans. According to the Kauffman Foundation, 360 out of 100,000 Americans start a business in any given month. Yet among Hispanics, this figure rises by 50 percent to 540 per 100,000 each month. Federal Reserve data indicates Latinos are 70 percent more likely to become entrepreneurs than non-Hispanic

Americans. According to a Hispanic Wealth survey, 24 percent of Latinos plan to start a business within the next five years, more than twice as many as their white counterparts.

The number of Hispanic business owners has grown 34 percent over the last ten years, making them by far the fastest-growing entrepreneurial subset. Hispanic-owned businesses with at least one employee are growing approximately twice as fast as the US average.

The Brookings Institution found that minorities are especially entrepreneurial in creating new online microbusinesses. Black owners make up 26 percent of all new enterprises, up from 15 percent before the pandemic. A recent National Bureau of Economic Research paper found a dramatic increase in new businesses in 2019 and 2020 in ordinary black neighborhoods.

In total, there are approximately ten million minority-owned small businesses in America, generating about $2 trillion of annual wealth and employing about ten million people. Their contribution to the US GDP is projected to triple between 2020 and 2060. Minority business payrolls and gross receipts are growing about five times faster than white businesses.

Despite these impressive numbers, overall levels of minority entrepreneurship indicate there's a lot of room for growth. Black people make up 14 percent of the American population yet just 2.3 percent of its employer firms and 11.8 percent of its non-employer firms. Hispanics make up 18 percent of the population yet just 6 percent of its employer firms and 14.7 percent of its non-employer firms.

Minorities can quickly close these entrepreneurship gaps and punch above their weight as long as we preserve the American entrepreneurship ecosystem based on free markets and limited government.

ENTREPRENEURSHIP ALSO BENEFITS
MINORITIES WHO DON'T CHOOSE IT

Entrepreneurship also benefits those people who have no other way to make a living. The unfortunate reality is that some Americans are nearly unemployable. These Americans, who are disproportionately minorities, often have disabilities, criminal records, or lack a high school education, making it difficult—if not impossible—to find traditional employment. These workers don't necessarily choose entrepreneurship; rather, they rely on it as a lifeline because they have no other options.

Bad public policy—such as $15 per hour entry-level wage requirements, failing public schools, occupational licensing requirements, and a criminal justice system that has overpenalized drug use—make it even more difficult for many disadvantaged Americans to gain a toehold on the employment ladder. Yet just because these minorities must use entrepreneurship as a last resort doesn't make their stories or the benefits of entrepreneurship any less powerful.

According to the Kauffman Foundation, about one in five American entrepreneurs are entrepreneurs by necessity. The Kauffman data indicates that the share of entrepreneurs inspired by necessity is higher among black and Hispanic Americans.

Research by Kylie Jiwon Hwang at Stanford Business School demonstrates that ex-convicts, disproportionately minorities, are "pushed into entrepreneurship as an alternative career choice to find work and gainful income." Even though this population didn't choose this path, entrepreneurship nevertheless helps them overcome racial economic disparities.

This "necessity entrepreneurship" can help minorities land jobs even if their ventures aren't successful. According to Hwang's research, "Entrepreneurship offers a bridge for formerly incarcerated individuals to secure employment that would otherwise have been impossible without an entrepreneurial experience."

"Employers perceive post-discrimination entrepreneurship as a signal of greater motivation and competence, and this signal also alleviates concerns regarding fit and commitment," writes Hwang. Greater ex-convict employment "holds regardless of entrepreneurial performance and is particularly true for subgroups that are even more discriminated against by employers, such as high school dropouts. ..."

ENTREPRENEURSHIP, NOT PROGRESSIVES' "STRUCTURAL" REFORMS, CAN IMPROVE RACIAL ECONOMIC EQUALITY

As academic research and the stories of heroes like Carlton demonstrate, entrepreneurship is the key to closing racial economic gaps—even when entrepreneurs don't succeed or intend to choose this path. The data shows that minority entrepreneurs have already closed racial income and wealth gaps that progressives claim only "structural" reforms can bridge.

A true commitment to boosting entrepreneurship and removing the barriers to starting small businesses can close racial economic gaps nationwide. Unfortunately, progressives misdiagnose racial economic inequality as a product of racism, leading them to pursue ineffective alternative policy responses that regulate and redistribute wealth rather than create it. This misguided path threatens to not only impede minority entrepreneurship gains but reverse them as well.

CHAPTER 2: RACIAL ECONOMIC DIFFERENCES ARE NOT DUE TO RACISM

It's one of the most viral political interviews in history: psychologist Jordan Peterson vs. Cathy Newman from Britain's Channel 4 News. This January 2018 debate over the gender pay gap has amassed more than forty million views on YouTube. Tucker Carlson called it one of the greatest interviews in history.

Newman repeatedly tries to back Peterson into a corner by starting her questions with "So you're saying that ..." followed by some sexist premise such as "women need to just accept that they're never going to make it on equal terms." Peterson deftly avoids her traps and explains that earnings differences between the sexes are not the result of sexism but rather numerous factors such as female career and education choices. One of the biggest reasons why women on average earn less, he explains, is that women are generally more agreeable than men, and compensation negotiation can be a contentious process.

"Multivariate analyses of the pay gap indicate that it doesn't exist ... If you're a social scientist worth your salt, you never do a univariate analysis. You say women, in aggregate, are paid less than men.

Okay. Well then we break it down by age; we break it down by occupation; we break it down by interest; we break it down by personality."

Peterson is directly countering the myth that gender earnings differences are a result of sexism, yet his logic also applies to the pervasive fiction that racial economic differences are a direct result of racism. Just as there are numerous reasons other than sexism why women, in aggregate, earn less than men, so there are many reasons other than racism why some minority groups make less than their white counterparts.

AMERICAN ELITES BELIEVE THAT RACIAL DIFFERENCES ARE DUE TO RACISM

To make the case that entrepreneurship offers minorities the best opportunity to overcome racial economic disparities, we first must destroy the widespread canard that these racial differences are the result of outright racism. If the racist justification is true, there's little that minorities can do to close the economic gaps, because the countervailing force of racism will thwart their progress.

This explanation, that racism is the primary force to blame, is accepted in seemingly all American institutions, from higher education to corporations, politics, and entertainment. Recall the self-flagellation in Hollywood after activists highlighted how Academy Awards predominantly went to white recipients and started their #OscarsSoWhite trend. (*Black Panther* was even nominated for Best Picture!)

Consider how many major American companies have implemented "equity" and anti-racism programs that prioritize race over merit for hiring and promotions in response to claims of minority underrepresentation. According to the World Economic Forum, one-third of Fortune 1000 companies have made public statements on racial equity.

Racial equity has infected nearly every college humanities course, even the hard sciences. California recently proposed new math curriculum that calls for an end to homework and even objective answers because they're supposedly "racist." The evidence that American elites believe racism is the reason for racial inequality—hence, that anti-racist policies are needed as a remedy—is all around us.

But is it true? Admittedly, racism still exists, and it likely always will in some small way. Studies show, for instance, that job applicants with traditionally black names are less likely to receive interview call-backs than applicants with traditionally white names even if they have the same qualifications.

However, the most recent large-scale study of this kind, conducted by the University of Chicago and the University of California Berkeley, found that the racial callback difference was only 2.1 percentage points. These studies have also been criticized for using stereotypically "poor" names for black applicants and stereotypically "wealthy" names for white applicants, thus muddying the results.

Nevertheless, I respect the experiences of minorities who have told me they have faced racism, and I admit it may play a small role in racial economic differences today. I have been on the receiving end of racism myself. When I went into a luxury car dealership to test drive a new model, for instance, the manager refused my request because he assumed I couldn't afford it.

(As an aside, I recognize that Latinos are not a "race" but an ethnicity with members of all different racial backgrounds. Same story for Middle Easterners. Yet in these hyper-racial times, Latinos like me are considered "people of color," so I will reluctantly accept that premise in this book.)

THE CATCH-22 IN ARGUING AGAINST SYSTEMIC RACISM

Upon closer inspection, it's clear that racism is not a systemic reason for racial disparities. In fact, I find it offensive when people claim it is the basis for minorities' economic challenges. Other minorities should, too.

These days in America, racism is sporadic, not systemic. Racism is universally viewed as one of the worst characteristics a person can have. Activists invoke it so often because it is such an effective cudgel. They have succeeded in implementing a Catch-22: to argue against systemic racism is, in itself, racist! This trap is one reason why the fiction that racism is the cause of racial inequality has been able to fester. Few are brave enough in this environment to argue against it.

I bear the battle scars. In the spring of 2022, I testified in front of the House of Representatives Ways and Means Committee on the topic of minority entrepreneurship and argued that minorities can overcome racial economic gaps through entrepreneurship. This perspective was in stark contrast to the other witnesses, who claimed the government needed to increase income redistribution to minorities to make up for the racism holding minorities back.

My testimony, based on years of research and expertise as the leader of one of the nation's largest small business groups, wasn't received well by the Democratic members, to put it lightly. Stacey Plaskett, delegate to the House from the US Virgin Islands, said she was "troubled by the rhetoric" she was hearing and claimed that it was "inappropriate" to argue minorities can overcome their circumstances through entrepreneurship.

Similarly, a few weeks before my testimony, Dina Rubio, a Florida restauranteur and member of the Job Creators Network, testified before the House about the barriers facing minority entrepreneurship. She argued that the government should do less, not more, pointing out the negative economic effects of government spending and regulations on her business. The hearing committee chair, Representative Jim Himes (D-CT), wasn't receptive to this message. He indicated that he was "disappointed" Rubio brought up this real-world problem, noting that he'd prefer to stick to supposed "structural" racial equity barriers facing entrepreneurs.

THERE'S NO REASON TO BELIEVE RACIAL ECONOMIC OUTCOMES SHOULD BE EQUAL

The evidence is clear. When all factors are considered, racism is not to blame for racial economic differences. In his powerful book *Discrimination and Disparities*, economist Thomas Sowell discusses the many "prerequisites" required for success and how the absence of these qualities—not racism—is the main driver of economic gaps between different populations.

"Morally neutral factors such as crop failures, birth order, geographic settings, or demographic and cultural differences," Sowell explains, "are among the many reasons why economic and social outcomes so often fail to fit the preconception of equal or comparable outcomes."

Given the wide variety of prerequisites needed for success, it's no surprise that the resulting outcomes are not randomly or distributionally allotted based on any one metric, like race. Sowell highlights research on the relative success of first-born children to demonstrate the folly of believing in equal outcomes. For instance, a study of National Merit Scholarship finalists showed that firstborns make up a majority of finalists in multichild families. Another example: of the original twenty-nine Apollo program astronauts, twenty-two were firstborn or only children.

"Consider how many things are the same for children born to the same parents and raised under the same roof—race, the family gene pool, economic level, cultural values, educational opportunities, parents' educational and intellectual levels, as well as the family's relatives, neighbors and friends—and yet the difference in birth order alone has made a demonstrable difference in outcomes ... If there is not equality of outcomes among people born to the same parents and raised under the same roof, why should equality of outcomes be expected—or assumed—when conditions are not nearly so comparable?"

THE REAL REASONS FOR RACIAL DISPARITIES

Considered analyses of racial disparities reveal a multitude of causes other than racism. Take, for instance, differences in entrepreneurial success. There is near consensus among entrepreneurship experts that a major factor in racially disparate business success rates is the lack of access to credit for minority entrepreneurs. These different funding outcomes by race, they seem to universally argue, stem from racist financial policies. For instance, economist William Michael Cunningham claims, "We were shocked by the layers of racism, discrimination, and anti-black behavior on the part of financial institutions and how that conspired to lower black business activity."

It's true that black and Hispanic Americans access credit at lower rates than white entrepreneurs. But could there be reasons for this disparity other than race? Indeed, multivariate analyses reveal that business size—not race—usually accounts for much of this difference in funding rates.

All small businesses have a more difficult time accessing credit than their big-business competitors, but the smallest of small businesses, disproportionately run by minorities, have an even harder time. Their lack of capital access is not due to racism but rather lending standards that require certain levels of profits, sales, employees, and intellectual property before loans can be offered. Small businesses, no matter their owner's race, often have to bootstrap their way to success.

Democrats actually made it even harder for small businesses to access credit in 2010 when the Dodd-Frank financial legislation decimated community banks around the country. For several years after the law's passage, one community bank would close every day, on average, across the country, culminating in a roughly 25 percent decline in the number of community banks nationwide.

The demise of small banks has big implications. Community banks are the lifeblood of towns across the country, providing the loans that big banks will not. These are the loans made on personal relationships, local knowledge, and a handshake—something that no loan algorithm can match. Small banks possess only 10 percent of the industry's assets but make one-quarter of the country's commercial loans, two-thirds of its small business loans, and three-quarters of its agricultural loans. Their disappearance has made it significantly more difficult for small businesses to access the start-up capital they need to succeed, especially for minority-owned businesses, which tend to be smaller.

Sowell points to data showing that black Americans are denied mortgages at twice the rate of whites. As in the case of racial differences in access to business credit, significant handwringing has occurred among politicians and commentators about how to fix this supposed "racial injustice." Yet what's generally not mentioned in this data is that whites, according to Sowell, are denied mortgages at nearly twice the rate of Asians. For the racist explanation to hold currency, loan officials must racially favor Asians over whites. Of course, looking at the analysis more deeply, the explanation for these racial divergences in mortgage lending is more prosaic: differences in credit scores. Those with lower credit scores, whether they're white or black, are less likely to be approved for a mortgage.

Similarly, today's racial disparities in incomes are often used as evidence of structural racism. The top quintile of households, which is disproportionately white and Asian, earned $141,110 or more in 2020 before taxes. The bottom quintile of households, which is disproportionately black and Latino, earned $27,026 or less before income transfers.

A more logical reason for this income divergence than racism is household structural differences that affect earnings. For instance, the number of workers per household, the number of hours worked per week, the age of household members, and married-couple families. (See chart below.)

Household Income by Characteristic in Top and Bottom Quintiles
Basic household characteristics, like hours worked, account for most of income inequality

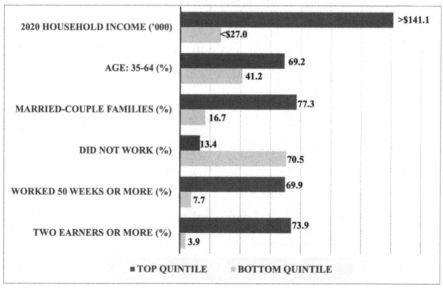

Source: Census Bureau – Income and Poverty in the United States, 2020; Income is before taxes and income transfers

The data reveals that most people in the bottom income quintile didn't work at all. In contrast, those in the top quintile work way more, both in terms of hours and people in the household working. It's no surprise that households with two or more earners working long hours earn significantly more than those with no one working, or just one person working part-time.

Yet another simple contributing factor: working-age members of households in the top quintile are far more likely to be in prime-age stages of their careers, meaning they have had longer to develop their skills and careers than those in the bottom quintile. Nearly 70 percent of those in the top quintile are between the ages of 35 and 64, versus just over 40 percent in the bottom quintile. Work output and experience may not generate headlines, but they are far more likely causes of racial economic inequality than racism.

In fields where minorities dominate, the logic also works in the opposite direction. When it comes to racial disparities in the National Basketball Association, the relevant metric isn't race; height, athleticism, and skill are the main reasons why black Americans dominate the NBA. Similarly, Asian outperformance in analytical fields isn't a result of racism but is largely due to studiousness.

DISPARATE OUTCOMES *WITHIN* RACIAL GROUPS INDICATE RACISM IS NOT THE CAUSE OF RACIAL DISPARITIES

Dramatic economic disparities within racial groups are perhaps the best evidence that racism is not the reason for wealth gaps. For instance, median Nigerian American households earned $68,658 in 2018, over 50 percent more than black Americans as a whole. Median Lebanese American households earned $87,099 on average in 2018, 30 percent more than Egyptian American households and 74 percent more than Moroccan American households. Median Argentine American households earned $75,810, similar to what Chilean and Bolivian American households earned. However, they made over 50 percent more than median Dominican or Honduran American households.

For these intra-racial wealth gaps to exist in the racist America of progressives' imaginations, people would have to hold racial animus toward some blacks but not others, to some Middle Easterners but not others, and some Latinos but not others. That's implausible.

In actuality, the biggest racial income gaps that exist in America are not between blacks and whites but among Asians from different backgrounds. A Pew Research report from 2018 revealed that Asians have the most racial income inequality, with the top 10 percent of earners making 10.7 times as much as the bottom 10 percent. Median household income among American households that list their race as Indian was $126,705 in 2019. Among those listed as Bangladeshi, household incomes were just a little over half that level at $67,944, and among Burmese households, only $45,903. (See chart below.)

Selected Median Household Incomes by Race/Ancestry
Significant income disparities within racial and ethnic groups undercut the racism justification for racial economic divides

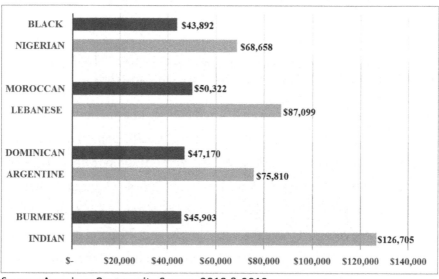

Source: American Community Survey, 2018 & 2019

How can this income fluctuation among races exist if the racism thesis were true? Simply put, it can't. Because racism is not the reason for racial differences, despite the prevalence of this contention.

Controlling for family formation indicates family is vital in determining economic outcomes. While the black poverty rate is well above the national average, the poverty rate among married blacks is below the rate of whites. Similarly, while black male labor force participation is below the national average, married black families participate in the labor force at higher rates than non-married whites.

Writes Sowell: "Do racists care whether someone black is married or unmarried? If not, then why do married blacks escape poverty so much more often than other blacks, if racism is the main reason for black poverty? If the continuing effects of past evils such as slavery play a major causal role today, were the ancestors of today's black married couples exempt from slavery and other injustices?"

When Assistant Secretary of Labor Daniel Patrick Moynihan published his famous report on the black family in 1965, 25 percent of black children were born out of wedlock. Today, that figure has increased to more than 75 percent. The research is clear: Growing up in a two-parent household helps children develop better socioeconomically than children in single-parent households. More than three-quarters of households in the top income quintile are married-couple families, versus just over one-sixth among the bottom quintile. The deterioration of family formation among racial minorities is likely another more significant driver of racial economic disparities than racism.

THE FREE MARKET IS BY FAR THE BEST ANTIDOTE TO THE REMAINING VESTIGES OF RACISM

Racism is clearly not the reason for racial economic differences. So, it stands to reason that further government programs designed to root out the last vestiges of racism will not help close racial economic gaps. A better approach would be to strengthen economic opportunities through the free market. Ironically, the very same free market that progressives want to curtail, regulate, and rule over in the name of addressing racism is the most potent antidote to racism.

While elites hawk the concept of "anti-racism"—the claim that we must implement racist policies to overcome traditional racism—the free market is actually anti-racist in the truest sense of the term. Capitalism financially punishes racial prejudice. The business owner who refuses to hire and promote people on merit, no matter their race, will soon fall behind his competitors who do. The entrepreneur who refuses to deal with suppliers who offer the best products at the best prices, independent of their race, will be outcompeted by those who do.

The American free-market economy is unique in that it brings people from all backgrounds together in a melting pot of economic success. People from countries and backgrounds where subjugation is common quickly learn to put away their historical animus in favor of economic success. Only under capitalism are people treated as individuals based on merit and productive capacity, not on immutable characteristics like race. As a result, America is one of the least racist countries in the world.

It's no surprise that racism is correlated with the amount of government control in a country. For instance, in France, where the government has far more control over the economy than in the United States, Arab minorities face racism in significant ways and often cannot get jobs in the country's notoriously regulated labor market. As a result, many languish in French slums known as *banlieues*.

As another example, India's rigid caste system consigns those born as "untouchables," who generally have darker skin, to a lifetime of poverty. Even today, about half the members of this caste work in sanitation because they are believed to be impure. China sends its Muslim minority, Uyghurs, to labor camps where they are often tortured and sterilized. It hardly needs repeating that the worst examples of racism in history were committed by the totalitarian governments of Nazi Germany and Soviet Russia.

Race merchants and Democratic politicians threaten the incredible anti-racist force of the free market with their racial equity proposals. Their desired programs, such as race reparations, affirmative action programs, racial government contracts, employment quotas by race, etc., would turn the country into the racist dystopia they claim already exists. Socialist policies abrogate individual rights—i.e., true protections for the smallest minority—to competing pressure groups fighting each other over the redistribution of resources.

Recommitting the country to capitalism will close racial gaps in two ways. First, it will create a vibrant economy that allows entrepreneurs to fulfill their dreams. Second, it will eliminate racial animus by treating people as individuals, not merely representatives of racial groups. Those who sacrifice capitalism in an effort to attain greater racial economic equality will get neither; those who prioritize the free market will get both.

CHAPTER 3: AMERICA'S MINORITY ENTREPRENEURSHIP ADVANTAGE

"*Expropiese!*"

That's the favorite word of countless socialist leaders in Latin America. By merely uttering "Expropriate it!" they steal small businesses in their countries and turn their local entrepreneurs' dreams into nightmares.

The Venezuelan reality TV show *Alo Presidente*, which followed former Venezuelan President Hugo Chavez around as he governed, was all too real for Venezuelan entrepreneurs. It depicts Chavez routinely pointing to small businesses he'd like the state to own and declaring "*Expropiese!*" met with uproarious applause from his entourage. It became his catchphrase.

In one representative clip, Chavez asks a local party apparatchik in Spanish, "That building there, what is it?"

The official responds that it houses "privately-owned jewelry stores."

Chavez says, "*Expropiese! Expropiese!*" Then he continues, "And that building on the corner?"

"That building also has local businesses."

"*Exprópiese*! *Exprópiese*! *Exprópiese*! We have to transform."

And just like that, small businesses that represented lifetimes of work simply vanished. Such direct government theft of property is shocking to American sensibilities, but this is commonplace in socialist states. And in developing countries around the globe, social democrats indirectly steal entrepreneurs' small-business output through oppressive taxation.

Is it any wonder why entrepreneurs worldwide have immigrated to the United States, where their business dreams can become reality?

Dina Rubio, owner of Don Ramon restaurant in West Palm Beach, Florida, has experienced this socialist hell firsthand. When she was seventeen, she and her family fled the 1979 Sandinista uprising in Nicaragua. Like all socialist regimes, the Sandinistas had brutally repressed anyone they considered bourgeois in the name of equality.

"Despite the fact my parents had two or three jobs and made sacrifices to send us to a private school," Dina recounts, "we were targeted."

The Sandinistas followed the tried and tyrannical socialist playbook, nationalizing the economy, stealing private property, destroying the currency, enacting price controls, conducting mass surveillance, and imprisoning and executing their opposition.

"This caused widespread shortages, hyperinflation, hunger, suffering, poverty, and oppression," Dina explains. Unsurprisingly, their socialist approach did not reduce inequality.

The Sandinista regime, like many iterations of socialist governance on the continent, received support from American progressives despite the obvious economic ruin they wrought. For instance, Senator Bernie Sanders (I-VT), who twice nearly earned the Democratic Party's presidential nomination, was asked by a journalist in the 1980s about the breadlines in Latin America caused by socialist policies. He responded,

"That's a good thing. In other countries, people don't line up for food. The rich get the food, and the poor starve to death."

Socialists' much-vaunted literacy programs—which Western progressives like Sanders, former New York City Mayor Bill de Blasio, and Canadian Prime Minister Justin Trudeau have effusively praised—were simply a means to spread regime propaganda to the countryside.

Dina and her family gave up their entire lives to pursue freedom and opportunity in the United States. "Life wasn't easy in the US," she recalls. "But the sacrifices were small compared to the chance to live in a free, democratic country. I was able to fulfill my parents' dream of going to college. I graduated with a bachelor's degree in interior design and was fortunate to work in my profession for eleven years."

In school, Dina met her future husband, Juan, who had escaped from socialist repression in Cuba. "He had the vision of someday having his own business—something that is difficult to impossible in socialist countries," says Dina. "He was driven and ambitious, which I admired in a young man. So, we partnered up for life."

America has long been a beacon for minority immigrants fleeing socialist governments around the world. America's entrepreneurship advantage has provided a lifeline to tens of millions of families over the years, including mine.

IMMIGRATION SHOWS AMERICA ISN'T RACIST AND HAS A MINORITY ENTREPRENEURSHIP ADVANTAGE

The best proof of American exceptionalism is the fact that hundreds of millions of immigrants have voluntarily chosen to come to this country. The overwhelming majority of recent immigrants are racial minorities. By choosing the United States, they demonstrate that this country is not plagued by racism that prevents economic advancement. If the United States were the racist country that progressives claim it is, immigrants would go to a different country, or merely enter America en route to Canada—something that never happens.

According to Gallup polling, nearly 150 million people (approximately 4 percent of the world's adult population) would move to the United States if they could. That figure is larger than the next four most popular destinations *combined*. Roughly one-third of all Hondurans and Dominicans want to come to America.

A Pew Research study showed that Asia has displaced Latin America as the biggest source of immigrants to the United States, demonstrating that immigrants don't merely choose this country because it's close. Asians are skipping over Europe, Canada, Australia, and numerous other closer countries and actively choosing the United States. Would they do this if America were plagued by structural racism that prevents minorities from succeeding?

Minorities pick the United States because it's where they can fulfill their dreams and live their best lives. In America, their lives are their own, not a tool of the state. Minority immigration both demonstrates America's entrepreneurship advantage and helps bolster it.

In recognition of the opportunity America offers, immigrants are disproportionately entrepreneurial. According to the Kauffman Foundation, immigrants start businesses 81 percent more often than the native-born population. A recent Massachusetts Institute of Technology study found that immigrant businesses create 42 percent more jobs than those run by the native-born population. "Immigrants, relative to natives and relative to their share of the population, found more firms of every size," confirms economist Pierre Azoulay, coauthor of the MIT study.

Census data stretching back 140 years reveals that immigrants are self-employed more often than native-born Americans. Immigrants account for almost 15 percent of the US population but make up nearly

30 percent of Main Street small businesses. Studies also show that immigrant entrepreneurs tend to be more innovative.

Minority immigrant entrepreneurs often start out with significant disadvantages, facing high financial, community, and language barriers. Their success shows the incredible opportunity for minorities of all backgrounds to close racial economic gaps through entrepreneurship. If penniless minority immigrants like Dina can make it, almost anyone can.

AMERICA'S ENTREPRENEURSHIP ADVANTAGE #1: HIGHER PAY AND LOWER TAXES

America has numerous entrepreneurship advantages over other countries that minorities can capitalize on to overcome racial disparities. The most obvious—and rarely discussed—benefit is the far higher pay that Americans earn.

Americans reap significantly higher financial rewards for their work than their counterparts around the globe. Middle-class Americans enjoy standards of living comparable with upper classes in other developed countries, and that would effectively make them rich in developing countries. Entrepreneurship is the best ticket to the American middle class.

American GDP per capita, one common measure of living standards, was $70,181 in 2021. This figure is 43 percent higher than the OECD average of $48,970. While these pay analyses do not control specifically for entrepreneurs, they do offer a good proxy to determine the relative financial rewards of American entrepreneurship versus other nations.

Yet this topline measure understates ordinary Americans' pay advantage, because it doesn't consider that Americans are also taxed far less than their developed-world peers. Middle-class Europeans face tax burdens nearly twice as large as what Americans encounter. As a result, America's advantage in take-home pay (what really counts) is even more significant.

The OECD finds that the average American annual household income after taxes (known as disposable income) is $51,147—68 percent more than the OECD average of $30,490. In Canada, disposable yearly household income is only $34,421. In France, it's just $34,375. (See chart below.) It's no wonder immigrants pass over these other countries for America.

Disposable Income in the US, OECD, Canada, and France
American disposable incomes are more than two-thirds higher than the OECD average

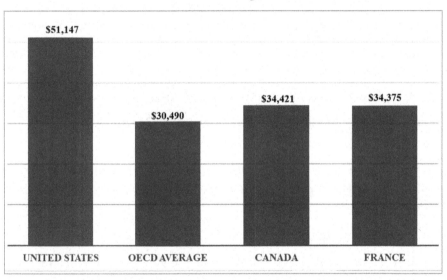

Source: OECD Better Life Index

Even this after-tax analysis understates the difference in disposable income between middle-class Americans and their peers from other developed nations, as it doesn't factor in sales tax paid on nearly all purchases. The average sales tax—often called a value-added tax—paid by Europeans is 22 percent. Meanwhile, the United States is the only OECD country with no federal sales tax, and the average state sales tax is 5 percent. When this regressive tax on purchases is factored into the analysis, ordinary Americans' living standards rise from 68 percent to approximately 75 percent higher than their OECD peers.

A 2017 Pew Research report examined the disposable household income of American and Western European middle-class households (those that earn between double and two-thirds their nation's median household income). It found that US after-tax incomes for these middle-class earners were approximately 50 percent higher than those in Western Europe.

The study revealed that many middle-class Europeans would be in a lower class if they lived in the United States, and many lower-class Americans would be in the middle class if they lived in Europe. A separate analysis published by *The Economist* shows that the bottom 10 percent of Americans would often be in the middle class or above if they lived in other OECD countries.

Due to America's highly progressive tax code, much of the American middle-class pays very low federal taxes. About 50 percent of American households pay no federal income tax at all. Nine states—including two of the biggest, Texas and Florida—have no state income tax at all. As mentioned, the United States is also the only developed nation without a regressive national sales or value-added tax. Unique among developed countries, America's government is funded almost entirely by the upper-middle class and wealthy. The top 5 percent of earners pay 60 percent of America's income taxes.

As a result of these tax advantages, American entrepreneurs can devote their earnings to financing and growing their businesses without being hamstrung by tax costs. This earnings advantage is one major reason why America is so entrepreneurial. The returns to entrepreneurship are just so much higher in the United States compared to anywhere else.

Unsurprisingly, when the rewards are greater, more Americans want to be entrepreneurs. According to a survey cited by the Federal

Reserve Bank of St. Louis, more than 70 percent of Americans prefer to be entrepreneurs than work a traditional job, versus 46 percent in Western Europe and 58 percent in Canada. Babson College's Global Entrepreneurship Monitor concludes that America's entrepreneurship rate is about twice as high as Europe's. The United States has the most robust small-business economy in the world backed by an army of self-employed individuals living the American Dream.

Given America's dramatic advantage in living standards, it's evident why entrepreneurs want to come to America to harness this opportunity for financial freedom. This pay premium and light tax burden are two major reasons why American minorities can close racial economic disparities. When the returns on entrepreneurship are so much lower in other countries, closing this racial gap is much more difficult.

More money in the hands of ordinary people leads to a more dynamic economy than the state-run systems. There is more money on Main Streets, where it is stimulative, and less money sucked away to national capitals, where it funds political objectives that may or may not directly help communities from which it was taken.

Minority immigrants like Dina especially appreciate America's entrepreneurship advantage because it contrasts so starkly with their experiences in their socialist-run home countries that directly or indirectly (through heavy taxation) expropriate their businesses.

AMERICA'S ENTREPRENEURSHIP ADVANTAGE #2: FREE LABOR MARKETS

In 2015, *The New York Times* published a shocking story on European labor markets. The article detailed the existence of thousands of fake small businesses operating throughout Europe parallel to the real economy. These Potemkin companies include a furniture manufacturer, a pet store, a porcelain distributor, and a perfumery, yet all the products at these businesses are fake.

What's going on here? Reports the *Times*:

> These companies are all part of an elaborate training network that effectively operates as a parallel economic universe. For years, the aim was to train students and unemployed workers looking to make a transition to different industries. Now they are being used to combat the alarming rise in long-term unemployment, one of the most pressing problems to emerge from Europe's long economic crisis.

The article profiles Sabine de Buyzer, who "works" for one of these phantom companies in France. She had not been able to find a real job after two years of looking and hoped this experience would help her land one. "It's been very difficult," she tells the *Times*. "When you look for a long time and don't find anything, it's so hard. You can get depressed. You question your abilities. After a while, you no longer see a light at the end of the tunnel."

Julia Moreno, another worker at one of these faux companies, said long-term unemployment makes you feel alone. "There are moments when you think maybe you're worth nothing." She concludes, "People look at you and say … 'Why are you, an older person, trying to take a job from a young person?'"

What a difference from the American economy where a surplus of unfilled jobs is a significant economic problem. It's impossible to read this story without feeling overwhelming gratitude that we get to pursue entrepreneurship in the United States, where labor markets are vibrant and robust.

While Europe's economic situation has improved since this article was published, long-term unemployment is still a significant problem. Before the pandemic, almost half of unemployed Europeans were out of work for fifty-two weeks or longer. In the United States, just 21 percent of unemployed workers were jobless for twenty-seven weeks or more in 2019. Approximately half of new jobs in Europe are temporary contracts. European jobseekers both young and old have very little opportunity to find meaningful work compared to their counterparts in the United States.

One of the main reasons Europe has so little economic opportunity is because of its rigid labor laws that make it nearly impossible to fire someone. One of the scariest parts of starting or growing a business is hiring your first employee. Economics and common sense indicate that if small businesses are afraid that they won't be able to fire ill-fitting employees, they often won't hire them in the first place, reducing broader economic vitality.

America's free-labor markets are a major reason for its entrepreneurship advantage. Specifically, American entrepreneurs benefit from the country's general use of at-will employment, which allows employers to fire their employees for any reason as long as it's not a protected reason, such as firing an employee due to their race, gender, or disability. The United States is the only developed country with such a free-labor market standard.

Economist Richard Epstein explains that the benefits of at-will employment include freedom of association, flexibility, and lower hiring costs. He writes, "The flexibility afforded by the contract at will permits the ceaseless marginal adjustments that are necessary in any ongoing productive activity conducted, as all activities are, in conditions of technological and business change." Employers can quickly scale up their businesses as economic conditions allow without fearing that they won't be able to downsize if needed.

At-will employment allows entrepreneurs to immediately get rid of problematic or unneeded employees. It prioritizes employee merit over seniority, helping make businesses more productive and profitable. Many scholars point to at-will employment as a major reason for

Silicon Valley's success, but it's just as crucial for the success of the neighborhood drycleaner, convenience store, or online business.

Free-labor markets are especially beneficial to minority entrepreneurs looking to capitalize on the business cycle by starting companies in industries that are more "boom-and-bust" than established industries. Compared to law firms, accounting agencies, and investment funds, disproportionately minority-run small businesses in food services, fashion, and culture greatly depend on the ability to hire and fire employees quickly as trends change.

At-will employment is a significant advantage for minority entrepreneurs in America, as well as a key reason why entrepreneurship can help American minorities overcome racial economic disparities.

AMERICA'S ENTREPRENEURSHIP ADVANTAGE #3: AN ENTREPRENEURSHIP CULTURE

Carlos Gazitua is the owner of Sergio's Restaurant in Miami. Carlos's grandmother and mother founded Sergio's after fleeing Fidel Castro's Cuba and landing in America with nothing but the clothes on their backs and recipes for authentic Cuban food in their heads. Opening a restaurant was a way for the family to escape the factory floor and become financially independent.

"They cried a lot in the beginning because they didn't know the struggles it would take to run a restaurant," Carlos told me. "Through their sacrifices, Sergio's grew from a small sandwich shop to a community staple."

Carlos cites at-will employment and access to capital as two of America's major entrepreneurship advantages. "My mother was amazed that banks were willing to lend her money to scale up her business by opening multiple locations. Sergio's was able to grow to the point where it could employ family and friends who [had] also left

Cuba, providing opportunities for the community."

Carlos also highlights another major advantage in America: the country's culture of entrepreneurship. "There's a culture in America of independence, freedom, and taking risk. There's a culture that if you put your hard work in, your earnings are not to be shared."

Carlos contrasts America's reverence for entrepreneurship with the "tall poppy syndrome" in other countries, wherein successful entrepreneurs get cut down by government and society for standing apart from the rest. "In other countries, success brings shame and earnings must be shared in society. In other countries, you can't even open a business and if you do everything is taken by the government."

America's culture of entrepreneurship gives ordinary people the courage to pursue their dreams. In contrast to other countries where only the privileged have a realistic shot at entrepreneurship, almost anyone and everyone is encouraged to be an entrepreneur in America, no matter their background. A Babson University study found that 75 percent of American adults believe entrepreneurs receive high status in society—markedly higher than the twenty-three other "innovation-driven economies" examined.

This culture is especially beneficial to minorities who may not have the connections, capital, and class background to become entrepreneurs in other countries. Even entrepreneurial failure is paradoxically considered success in America, whereas in other countries it is an embarrassment. This culture inspires confidence in minorities from even the most challenging backgrounds to pursue their entrepreneurial dreams.

Carlos argues that minority entrepreneurship itself helps foster a pro-entrepreneurship culture. "Only through everyone's understanding of how hard it is to be successful will people appreciate success of others. When you're an entrepreneur, you appreciate successes of others because you know how hard it is."

He says that successful minority entrepreneurs are responsible for America's melting pot of assimilating cultures. He calls on minorities to "show their success" to indicate to younger generations that minority entrepreneurship success is possible, and that the economic system is not rigged the way progressives claim. "Entrepreneurship is the essence of the American Dream," Carlos concludes. "Successful small businesses ensure independence, assimilation, and freedom."

Many Americans don't recognize how equal economic opportunity truly is in this country, where success is based on merit and hustle, not intrinsic characteristics. This lack of appreciation results from progressives and their media trumpets producing a steady drumbeat of propaganda that the United States suffers from unacceptably high rates of inequality. Politicians use this media narrative as a justification to grow the size of government at the expense of entrepreneurs.

All the while, progressives and the media never mention that economic opportunity is far less equal in other countries. For instance, they conveniently ignore:

- The United Kingdom's entrenched class system, where economic success can come down to whether entrepreneurs have the proper English accent and where people are discouraged from venturing too far above their station.

- Canada's entrenched crony capitalist alliance between big corporations and big government that works to shut out entrepreneurial upstarts.

- Asia's hierarchical economic structure that rewards seniority and status over ingenuity and merit.

- France's preference for graduates from the country's top universities, known as *Grande Écoles*, over ordinary entrepreneurs who have stronger skills.

- The apprenticeship programs in Germany, Austria, and

Switzerland that are great for those who take part in them but also lock out hard workers and fast learners who weren't able to access them.

- The managerial capitalism that persists in every other developed country and subsumes entrepreneurs to the decisions of elite technocrats who believe they know best.

- The widespread and truly systemic racism that exists in almost every other country in the world, preventing minorities from getting ahead.

Only in America can people from any background achieve their entrepreneurial dreams. At the very least, they have a far better opportunity than their peers anywhere else in the world. That's America's most fundamental minority entrepreneurship advantage.

CHAPTER 4: HOW THE GOVERNMENT BLOCKS MINORITY ENTREPRENEURSHIP

Have you ever heard of a *lemon* mojito? Me neither. But it sure sounds bad.

Yet that's what Dina Rubio, who owns Don Ramon restaurant in West Palm Beach, Florida, has been forced to offer her customers in place of the traditional lime variety.

Why the drastic move? Runaway inflation.

"A box of limes that I used to be able to find for $30 now costs me $90," Dina tells me. "Wholesale steak prices have risen from $7 to $12."

In response to these dramatic price increases, Dina's been forced to raise menu prices just to remain profitable, alienating her loyal customers on fixed incomes who don't understand her predicament. "I've also had to keep some items off the menu entirely because they are no longer profitable to sell," she says. "I've needed to make product substitutions, like making mojitos with lemons, even if the taste is not as good."

Across the nation, minority small businesses are being forced to take similar drastic measures to deal with the highest inflation in forty-one years. According to the Bureau of Labor Statistics, consumer prices rose 9.3 percent between July 2021 and June 2022. Wholesale prices that small businesses pay increased even faster, at a rate of 11.3 percent, over that period. Anecdotal evidence suggests the inflation rate affecting small businesses is even higher still.

"Food prices are slamming local restaurants," reports *The Wall Street Journal*. "At GrandDaddy's Hot Chicken, located in [Nashville], a single tender—seasoned, fried, and coated with a cayenne pepper blend—costs $3. A year ago, it was $1.85."

Inflation-induced price increases have significant consequences for small businesses. Customers are price sensitive. There's only so much someone will be willing to spend on a chicken tender, mojito, or dry-cleaned shirt before they simply stay home. Approximately 30 percent of drycleaners, which are often run by minorities, have gone out of business since the pandemic, as they haven't been able to pass their higher costs on to their customers on fixed incomes.

"Technically, I should have raised stuff a long time ago, but I can't, because people are not going to want to buy," said GrandDaddy's black owner, Tommy Buchanan. He notes that the price of a 40-pound case of tenders has doubled over the past year, forcing him to take wings completely off the menu.

"The case of chicken used to be, like, forty bucks—now it's one hundred twenty and keeps going up and up," says Gerson Velasquez, owner of Half-Moon Bakery in Cleveland, whose empanadas are a community staple. "We're barely making enough to pay the employees, and that's something that's a little scary."

Velasquez explains he doesn't want to raise prices on his customers, because he understands his bakery's role in feeding the community. But in the end, he has no choice. "I'm going to keep fighting and try to survive because that's what we've been doing the last few years with the pandemic. Now with the gas prices, we just have to try to survive."

America has a unique minority entrepreneurship advantage, but the government continually threatens it with bad public policy. Minority entrepreneurship and its power to overcome racial economic differences are hamstrung by these bad government actions. Runaway inflation as a result of reckless spending is Exhibit A.

Record high gas prices due to radical green policy, stiff restrictions on business activity during the Covid-19 pandemic, overregulation (such as occupational licensing requirements), and barriers to accessing capital are among other prime examples.

Bad government policy disproportionately impacts small business owners. Small businesses generally don't have the economies of scale, preferential purchasing agreements, or profit margins that their big-business competitors do. Small businesses have almost no protection from the costs imposed by bad policy. This dynamic is especially true for minority-owned small businesses, which tend to be even smaller and less profitable.

RECKLESS GOVERNMENT SPENDING FUELS INFLATION, THE ENEMY OF MINORITY SMALL BUSINESSES

The Job Creators Network's SBIQ polling of national small business owners indicates that today's high inflation is by far the biggest issue facing entrepreneurs. (See chart below.) This crushing inflation is the direct result of reckless government spending after the nation had already begun recovering from the Covid-19 pandemic.

Biggest Concern of Small Businesses

Inflation dominates list of top concerns among small businesses

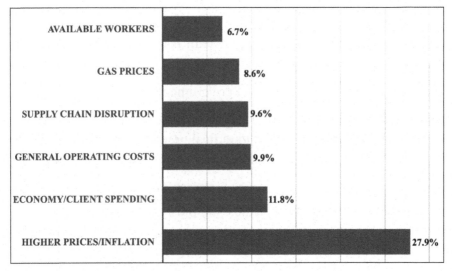

Source: Job Creators Network Foundation SBIQ Monthly Poll: Small Business Employers – Aug. 2022

At the beginning of 2021, I was among the first to warn that massive deficit spending threatened to dramatically inflate prices. Unfortunately, congressional Democrats and the Biden administration ignored bipartisan warnings about inflation and proceeded to jam through spending blowouts.

President Biden signed the $1.9 trillion American Rescue Plan into law in March of 2021, when the economy was already recovering. He followed that up by signing a $1.1 trillion infrastructure-in-name-only bill in November 2021. Democrats were very close to passing the $5 trillion "Build Back Better" social spending bill, which would have turned today's high inflation hyper, but fortunately, vocal small-business backlash helped prevent it from passing.

Trillions of dollars of reckless spending overstimulated demand and led to too many dollars chasing too few goods, putting significant upward pressure on prices. This deficit spending was monetized by the

Federal Reserve when it started printing more money, devaluing the currency already in existence.

Nobel Prize-winning economist Milton Friedman explained, "Inflation is always and everywhere a monetary phenomenon, in the sense that it is and can be produced only by a more rapid increase in the quantity of money than in output."

On the campaign trail, Biden said, "Milton Friedman isn't running the show anymore." Talk about tempting fate. Friedman is having the last laugh now. Even presidents can't fight basic economics.

Today's inflation is the chit that's been looming due for years of fiscal profligacy and easy money that politicians have said is "cost-free." It's a black eye for Democrats, because it directly results from their Keynesian fiscal religion and Modern Monetary Theory madness.

Today's painful inflation should put a nail in the coffin of MMT, the belief held (at least in practice) by many Democrats that deficits don't matter, because money grows on trees—or at least on Federal Reserve printers. Indeed, the inflation cost of MMT is proving high and painful. This philosophy is also responsible for the federal debt hitting $32 trillion, the net interest on which threatens to be a massive drag on the economy moving forward.

The decreasing value of the dollar further discredits the big-government approach to managing the economy. Next time the government calls for some massive social spending program, small businesses will be wary. "We tried that approach already," Americans can say, "and it resulted in runaway inflation, falling real incomes, and decreased living standards."

Yet the discrediting of left-wing fiscal and monetary policy is cold comfort for today's small businesses picking up the bill today for Democrats' supposed free lunch of dramatic government spending.

RADICAL ENVIRONMENTAL POLICY RAISES GAS PRICES, INCREASING MINORITY SMALL BUSINESS COSTS

Antonio Urrianna runs a three-person landscaping business in Chicago. He estimates that he now spends $100 a day on gas for his truck and landscaping tools such as his mower.

Sky-high gas prices, averaging around $5 a gallon nationwide, are placing a heavy burden on minority small businesses, preventing both their creation and growth. Minority-owned small businesses are disproportionately impacted by high gas prices because they are far more likely to be involved in businesses that require transportation.

For many minority-owned small businesses, the name on the side of their truck is more important than the name on its front. In contrast, white workers and entrepreneurs are more likely to work from offices or at home and thus are more insulated from the consequences of high gas prices.

In Los Angeles, thousands of one-man landscaping businesses, seemingly all run by hardworking Hispanics, make the long commute into town every day from the Inland Empire, the working- and middle-class cities an hour or so east of LA. Facing gas prices upwards of $6 a gallon, these entrepreneurs are victims of bad government policy, paying hundreds of dollars a day in gas costs just to fill their trucks and tools.

This army of landscapers, which exists in most big American cities, often cannot simply pass these gas costs on to their customers in the form of higher rates. At a certain point, their middle-class customers, who are also looking to cut costs amid rising prices, will simply choose to do the yard work themselves.

Record gas prices, which approximately doubled between the beginning of 2021 and mid-2022, are devastating minority small business owners like Antonio Urrianna, who consume a lot of gas as a part of their businesses.

Even small businesses that don't involve a pickup truck or a work van are impacted by today's gas prices. Gas is an input cost in almost every good a small business uses; ordinary small businesses are also paying for record gas prices through higher supply costs. One poll from spring 2022 found that more than two out of three small business owners said high gas prices were having a "very significant" negative impact on their business.

Bad government policy is directly responsible for today's sky-high gas prices. The Biden administration's radical green rhetoric and policies have reduced the supply of fossil fuels, increasing their prices. On the campaign trail, Biden said, "I guarantee you we're going to end fossil fuels," and claimed his administration would make the country "transition away from the oil industry."

On Biden's first day in office, he canceled the Keystone XL Pipeline, which would have boosted fossil fuel supply from Canada. His administration banned drilling on federal lands. It enacted dozens of other regulations that reduced drilling and refining capacity, and it has furthermore increased fees and permit requirements. Biden has leased fewer acres of land for oil and gas drilling than any presidential administration in the past seventy-six years.

According to Katie Tubb, energy policy analyst at the Heritage Foundation, "The Biden administration's rejection of the Keystone XL pipeline was only the most visible" but hardly the only anti-oil action it has taken. "It also has proposed or finalized regulations that restrict nearly every aspect of the oil industry: financing and private-sector investment, exploration and production, pipeline construction and operation, and consumer use."

Bad policy reduced the oil supply and undid the energy independence won by Trump administration policies. Today, the nation is once again forced to ask Persian Gulf monarchs and South American dictators to boost oil production. Meanwhile, small businesses, especially those run by minorities, are paying the price in the form of $100 fill-ups that are destroying their profit margins.

COVID-19 GOVERNMENT LOCKDOWNS DISPROPORTIONATELY HURT MINORITY SMALL BUSINESSES

Patrice Graham opened the first black-owned yoga studio in Raleigh, North Carolina, a few years ago. She had the dream of starting an inclusive yoga studio with small class sizes catering to those who felt out of place at other studios in town. Seven months into the Covid-19 pandemic, she had to close her studio for good, as state reopening plans kept getting pushed back.

Yvonne McNair owns Captivate Marketing Group, an organization that promotes the Essence Music Festival, an annual event over the Fourth of July weekend in New Orleans featuring some of the nation's most prominent black entertainers.

When Yvonne's 2020 schedule of events was almost entirely canceled due to government regulations on capacity gatherings, Yvonne had to fire all of her seven employees and twenty-five independent contractors. She estimates her business will lose 1.5 years' worth of income as a result.

Patrice and Yvonne are just two cases of approximately two hundred thousand small businesses that were forced to shut down due to Covid-19 and the ensuing state and local government restrictions.

Long after it was clear that businesses were not meaningful vectors of disease transmission, and long after it was clear that lockdowns did not significantly reduce Covid-19 infection rates, governments and local health officials continued to impose draconian restrictions on business activity. These governments effectively outlawed many forms of entrepreneurship. Less strict regulations often took the form of "hygiene theater," requiring businesses to perform various sanitization and spacing functions of little to no value but at an expensive cost.

Adding insult to injury, Covid-19 business restrictions were mostly pushed by politicians and bureaucrats whose paychecks were not affected in the slightest by business closures and embraced by the professional class who could easily pivot their jobs to Zoom. Never consulted in the business restriction debate were the actual small business owners—often minorities—whose livelihoods were sacrificed to supposedly save lives.

Restaurants, barbershops, dry cleaners, bodegas, and other retailers disproportionately run by minority entrepreneurs bore the brunt of the business restriction pains. These businesses cannot operate solely with a Wi-Fi connection. As a result, black-owned businesses fell by 41 percent and Latino-owned businesses by 32 percent in the months following the pandemic, versus about a 20 percent drop among small businesses overall.

According to an H&R Block survey of nearly three thousand small businesses, 53 percent of black business owners saw their revenue drop by half, versus 37 percent of white owners, in the aftermath of the pandemic.

In states like California, restrictions on business activity ran through most of 2021—well after vaccines had been introduced and it was clear that lockdown costs far exceeded their negligible benefits. Many minority entrepreneurs responded to these restrictions by leaving California altogether for free states like Florida and Texas.

But not all businesses can move states or move online. Some of them had no other choice but to close. They are the other casualties of the Covid-19 pandemic. It was not the virus that killed them–it was bad government policy.

GOVERNMENT OVERREGULATION DISPROPORTIONATELY HURTS MINORITY SMALL BUSINESSES

Ashley N'Dakpri runs Afro Touch, a hair-braiding salon in Louisiana. She wants to hire more stylists to meet demand, but Louisiana's strict occupational licensing regulations prevent her from doing so.

Ashley legally isn't allowed to hire new stylists unless they have a cosmetologist's license, a certification that requires five hundred hours of training and thousands of dollars in fees to obtain. She notes that many potential employees are no longer interested in working for her once they discover the onerous occupational licensing requirements.

State-level occupational licenses are a major barrier to minority entrepreneurship. These licenses prevent many minorities from starting their own businesses in fields across the economic spectrum. Occupational licenses are *de facto* laws against minority entrepreneurship.

The beauty industry is perhaps the most egregious example of a field whose occupational licensing requirements prevent minority entrepreneurship, but these licenses are also found in many other industries popular with minority entrepreneurs, including construction, childcare, and pest control.

Cosmetology licenses are often far more difficult to get than licenses for professions that deal with life and death. In Massachusetts, for instance, cosmetologists must complete one thousand hours of coursework and two years of apprenticeship before they are allowed to ply their trade in the beauty industry. Emergency medical technicians, by contrast, must only take 150 hours of courses to be allowed to work.

What are these occupational licenses protecting consumers from? A bad hair day? These permits present an enormous entrepreneurial barrier to mostly minority women. According to a study by the Institute of Justice, Louisiana has just thirty-two licensed African hair braiders.

In stark contrast, neighboring Mississippi, which has approximately four hundred thousand fewer black residents but doesn't regulate hair braiding, has 1,200.

California is the worst occupational licensing offender, according to IJ, putting up "a nearly impenetrable thicket of bureaucracy." Basic trades such as door repair, carpentry, and landscaping require potential entrepreneurs to devote 1,460 days to supervised practice and spend up to thousands of dollars for a license before they can legally work.

Nearly one-quarter of American workers hold a license, according to the Labor Department, up from about 5 percent in the 1950s. Unsurprisingly, a Federal Reserve Bank of Minnesota report concluded that minorities are significantly less likely to hold a license than whites. Research by economist Stephen Slivinski indicates that licensing requirements reduce minority entrepreneurship. He finds that states that require more occupational licenses have lower rates of low-income entrepreneurship.

Occupational licenses are just one example of bad government regulation. Small businesses face a regulatory onslaught of rules that produce death by one thousand cuts. Cato Institute economist Chris Edwards explains the regulatory maze facing small businesses from all levels of government:

> The federal government imposes regulations on businesses related to occupational health and safety, environment, wages and overtime, health and retirement benefits, family leave, workplace harassment and discrimination, disability, immigration and employment eligibility, labor unions, privacy, antitrust, truth in advertising, foreign trade, and many other areas.

> State governments impose business regulations related to health care, the environment, workers' compensation, occupational licensing, minimum wages, and other activities, and

they have a large role in regulating certain industries, such as utilities and alcohol.

Local governments impose regulations related to land use, zoning, business permitting, and other activities.

For many businesses, the addition of Covid-19 health and capacity regulations was the final straw that broke the camel's back.

University of Chicago economist Steven J. Davis explains how regulations disproportionately harm small businesses in three primary ways: "First, there are fixed costs of regulatory compliance. ... Second, there are one-time costs of learning the relevant regulations, developing compliance systems, and establishing relationships with regulators. ... Third, compared to smaller, newer, and would-be competitors, larger and incumbent firms have greater capacity and incentive to lobby for legislative exemptions, administrative waivers, and favorable regulatory treatment."

These regulatory hurdles are even higher for those run by minorities.

GOVERNMENT BARRIERS TO CREDIT MAKE IT MORE DIFFICULT FOR MINORITY SMALL BUSINESSES TO ACCESS THE CAPITAL THEY NEED TO GROW

After a brutal period during the Covid-19 pandemic, American small businesses were poised to take advantage of pent-up consumer demand. Many small businesses were looking to scale up to leverage this opportunity by taking out loans to increase supply and capacity.

Access to credit is often necessary for small business owners looking to start and grow their businesses, and that is especially true for minority small businesses.

According to a 2022 survey by Goldman Sachs, nearly 30 percent of American small business owners planned to take out a loan during the year, and 31 percent of them were confident in their ability to access credit. In contrast, 48 percent of black-owned businesses planned to borrow during the year, and only 19 percent were confident in their ability to do so.

Congressional Democrats and the Biden administration have made it far more difficult for these businesses to access the credit they need. In June 2021, the administration repealed President Trump's "true lender" rule that defined the regulatory requirements and compliance obligations between banks and the growing number of innovative online third-party lenders known as "fintech."

The "true lender" rule clarified that banks are generally the real lenders when they partner with intermediaries to offer loans. This rule was needed to harness and provide regulatory certainty for the growing number of app-based lenders that make up the fintech revolution. Nearly fifty economists and financial scholars noted that repealing this rule would hurt secondary lending markets and reduce access to credit.

This attack on access to credit followed the Obama administration's curtailment of capital as part of the 2010 Dodd-Frank financial regulations that decimated the nation's community banks via compliance costs. Community banks provided about 50 percent of the nation's small business loans, and as they have disappeared, so have credit opportunities for small businesses.

Since the passage of Dodd-Frank, more than 1,700 banks have shut down—accompanied by relatively few new bank formations. In Wyoming, for instance, the number of FDIC-insured banks has fallen by nearly half since 2000.

Fintech has stepped in to fill these banking deserts, helping small businesses access loans that big banks generally don't offer. These twenty-first-century lenders make loan origination easier and more consumer-friendly. They increase credit options for small businesses, especially those from underbanked minority communities.

The "true lender" rule also would have helped community banks themselves, as they often can't afford to acquire the personnel and infrastructure needed to offer the wide range of financing options required by consumers. According to a survey by the consultancy Cornerstone Advisors, two-thirds of banks and three-quarters of credit unions said fintech partnerships are important to their business strategies. Reversing the rule has put further financial pressure on community banks across the country, further entrenching big banks' power.

So, why do Democrats oppose this rule? They claimed it weakened consumer protections. Senator Chris Van Hollen (D-MD) stated that by issuing this rule, "The Trump administration ripped consumer protections to shreds, leaving Americans vulnerable to unscrupulous predatory lenders who charge outrageous interest rates."

Actually, the rule didn't alter consumer protection laws; rather, it allowed lenders to extend credit to those limited to more expensive payday or title loan lenders. Fintech fills a vital gap between these non-bank lenders and major financial institutions.

Curtailing access to credit for these businesses by repealing the "true lender" rule makes it even more difficult for small businesses to acquire the funding they need to scale and grow. It also threatens the broader fintech revolution that holds the power to dramatically expand credit options for minorities.

Whether it comes in the form of inflation, high gas prices, Covid-19 business restrictions, overregulation, or reduced access to credit, minority small businesses face a multifront attack from bad government policy. Big government actions such as reckless spending, radical green policies, health restrictions, occupational licensing, and attacks on fintech are the most significant hurdle preventing minority entrepreneurs from reducing racial economic disparities.

In short, the government is the biggest check on the country's minority entrepreneurship advantage—but that needn't be the case in perpetuity. By doing less, the government can transform from a minority entrepreneurship hindrance to a help.

CHAPTER 5: GOVERNMENT SHOULD DO LESS TO BOOST MINORITY ENTREPRENEURSHIP

To increase minority entrepreneurship, the government should do less, not more. Knocking down government barriers is the best way to bolster minority small businesses and accelerate the closure of racial economic gaps through entrepreneurship.

Consider the minority entrepreneurship boom that the 2017 Tax Cuts and Jobs Act produced. These tax cuts reinvigorated American small businesses, allowing entrepreneurs to compete on an even playing field with big companies for the first time. The tax cuts led to historic shared economic prosperity in 2018 and 2019, with minorities closing racial disparities at one of the fastest rates in modern history.

"Tax cuts delivered a new 20 percent small business tax deduction, allowing owners like me to protect one-fifth of our earnings to reinvest back into our businesses," explains Carlos Ruiz, owner of HT Metals in Tucson. "This tax relief lowers the effective top marginal tax rate for small business owners from 40 percent to 30 percent, strengthening the backbone of the American economy."

Like countless minority small business owners, Carlos used the additional funds from the tax cut to expand his business, purchase new equipment, and improve wages and benefits for his employees. "Multiply similar actions across the nation's thirty million small business owners," explains Carlos, "and you get a better understanding of how tax cuts [fuel] economic fire."

Small business tax cuts give entrepreneurs the funds they need to make their business dreams a reality. Less well-capitalized minority small businesses are even bigger tax cut winners.

In addition to provisions such as the 20 percent deduction and immediate expensing on all business investments, these tax cuts indirectly benefit entrepreneurs. They allow more money to stay on Main Street, where it can stimulate local communities that need it, and less to disappear to Washington, DC, where it is so often wasted. More money in the hands of ordinary Americans created an enormous economic stimulus that boosted consumer demand, further helping small businesses. As Carlos puts it, the tax cuts "created more demand for the raw materials that I supply." The same story can be heard from minority entrepreneurs across the nation who saw their sales surge as a result of the tax cut stimulus.

Carlos Gazitua, the president of Sergio's Restaurant in South Florida, was able to use his tax cut savings to offer 401ks to all 650 of his employees. Dina Rubio, who runs Don Ramon restaurant in Palm Beach, used the savings from the tax cuts to build a full bar in her restaurant. Other minorities used their tax cut savings to take their businesses to the next level, from a side hustle to a full-time job or from an at-home basement project to a brick-and-mortar store.

TAX CUTS DIRECTLY HELP MINORITY ENTREPRENEURS THROUGH THE CREATION OF OPPORTUNITY ZONES

The Tax Cuts and Jobs Act also directly helped minority entrepreneurs through its provision allowing tax-free investments in so-called "Opportunity Zones"—distressed, mostly minority communities across the country that the economy has left behind. Fifty-seven percent of the 31.5 million Americans who live in OZs are non-white minorities. This OZ provision has funneled billions of dollars of investment into these communities, providing economic opportunities for minorities who need it most.

"Turning an eighty-three-year-old school into an assisted living facility. Building a 125-room teaching hotel on a college campus. Converting a downtown Birmingham building [that has been] vacant for four decades into loft apartments. Those are just three of about $1 billion in potential developments by private investors around Alabama," reports AL.com on how the OZ tax cut provision has unleashed investments in distressed areas throughout the state. "Each of the projects is located in poverty-stricken areas that, until recently, might have looked like risky investments for private developers."

Yet the tax cuts have tipped the investor calculus toward revitalizing these distressed minority parts of the state. OZs are expected to incentivize $100 billion worth of investments in these areas nationwide, providing countless minority entrepreneurs with the infrastructure and opportunity they need to succeed.

Taken together, the tax cuts produced historic shared prosperity that disproportionately benefitted minorities. The tax cuts caused the economy to surge. Real GDP increased 2.5 percent and 2.3 percent 2018 and 2019, respectively, faster than any other G7 nation.

In addition, the unemployment rate reached a fifty-year low and a record low for black, Hispanic, and Asian American workers. The labor force participation rate reversed its long decline and actually began to increase as the red-hot jobs market pulled Americans from all backgrounds, including ex-convicts, high-school dropouts, and those with disabilities, into the labor market.

Wages surged, including wages adjusted for inflation. In 2019, real median income rose by 7.9 percent for black households, 7.1 percent for Hispanics, 10.6 percent for Asian Americans, and 5.7 percent for whites. Each of these numbers represents record increases and record absolute rates.

Real Median Income Growth by Household Race/Ethnicity in 2019
Free-market policies that boost entrepreneurship disproportionately boost minority incomes

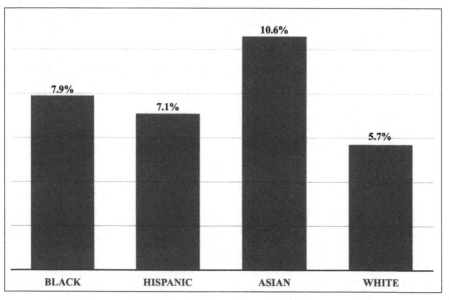

Source: Annual Report of the Council of Economic Advisers, Jan. 2021

Following the Tax Cuts and Jobs Act, wages grew 24 percent faster for Hispanics, 79 percent faster for blacks, and 95 percent faster for Asian Americans than during President Obama's second term. The Hispanic homeownership rate reached a record high. More than six million people were pulled from poverty, reducing the poverty rate to the lowest level in US history.

The widespread claim that these tax cuts only benefited the rich is fiction. The tax cuts created tangible measures of shared prosperity that helped ordinary workers more than the rich. They provided a larger tax reduction for the lowest-income Americans, who received a 10 percent cut, than the top 1 percent, who received less than a 0.5 percent cut. Real wages for the bottom 10 percent of earners grew nearly twice as fast as for the top 10 percent. The real wealth of the bottom 50 percent of households rose three times faster than that of the top 1 percent. Wages rose faster for workers than managers.

The tax cuts actually made the tax code more progressive, with the rich paying a larger share of total taxes. It eliminated the tax liability entirely for millions of American families.

Unfortunately, these tax cuts are set to expire at the end of 2025. The best action policymakers can take to help spur minority entre-preneurship is to make these tax cuts permanent. Doing so will give entrepreneurs cost certainty and allow them to make investments while feeling confident in their future returns.

Making these tax cuts permanent can directly help entrepreneurs like Carlos Ruiz continue growing their businesses. This action is the best way the government can do less, not more, to help minority entre-preneurs and close racial economic gaps.

JCN AMERICAN SMALL BUSINESS PROSPERITY PLAN WOULD BOOST MINORITY SMALL BUSINESSES

In the summer of 2022, JCN created its American Small Business Prosperity Plan in conjunction with former Speaker of the House Newt Gingrich. The plan includes public policies that legislators and all Americans should back to boost small businesses, including minority small businesses.

In addition to making tax cuts permanent, the contract would over-come many of the big government hurdles discussed in the last chapter.

For instance, the plan calls on legislators to support fiscal responsibility, including balancing the budget by stopping reckless spending that fuels the inflationary fire. It demands boosting domestic energy production, which will help increase fossil fuel supply and reduce runaway gas and energy prices burdening small businesses.

The plan supports exempting small businesses from new regulations that disproportionately hurt minority small businesses. It also calls for supporting access to credit such as fintech that minorities increasingly rely on to acquire the funds they need to establish and grow their businesses.

THE JOB CREATORS NETWORK AMERICAN SMALL BUSINESS PROSPERITY PLAN

1. **Make the Tax Cuts and Jobs Act Permanent**

   The 2017 Tax Cuts and Jobs Act unleashed a tsunami of small business expansion, leading to one of the strongest economies in half a century. But now, the legislation is set to incrementally expire and serve America's small business community what is effectively a tax hike. Congress should make small business tax relief permanent.

2. **Unleash Domestic Energy Production**

   High gas prices are a top concern for small businesses, as they currently face skyrocketing transportation costs they often cannot pass on to consumers. Congress should demand that the Biden administration unshackle the US oil industry so it can increase production and lower costs.

3. **Enact Healthcare Reform to Benefit Small Businesses and Families**

   The current healthcare system isn't working, as government

red tape and middlemen are inflating costs and restricting choice. Policymakers need to restore the doctor-patient relationship and remove DC bureaucrats and politicians from the exam room as well as increase healthcare choices, price transparency, and competition.

4. **Exempt Small Businesses from New Regulations**

   Handling the ever-growing mountain of government regulations put in place by Washington is a major hurdle for small business owners. Unlike large corporations, small businesses have a difficult time absorbing compliance costs often associated with government red tape. So, as a default, Main Street should be exempt from any new government regulations unless policymakers can prove that small businesses would not be disproportionately harmed by the change.

5. **Rein In Government Spending to Combat High Inflation**

   Out-of-control government spending is contributing to near-record inflation that acts as a punishing tax hike for small businesses. As the cost of input materials goes up, businesses can only pass along so much of the burden to consumers; small business budgets eat the rest. Congress should cut the budget and reallocate unused pandemic-era funds for targeted small business relief before even considering additional spending bills.

6. **Expand Access to Capital for Small Businesses**

   It's often difficult for small businesses to compete with their larger counterparts because of the challenges they face in accessing capital. Congress should explore strategies to open up capital markets more widely to small businesses so they can compete, innovate, and grow like their big business competitors.

7. **Reinstate Work Requirements for Recipients of Government Assistance**

Providing a reasonable government-funded safety net for Americans who fall on hard times is necessary. At the same time, we need to restore the dignity of work to help address lingering labor shortages that are compromising the US economy. Congress should tie work requirements to government assistance programs for able-bodied people—a proposal supported by 74 percent of Americans.

8. **Get Tough on China and Unclog Obstructed Supply Chains**

Chronic supply chain problems have been a massive headache for small businesses. Congress should investigate what government regulations can be lifted to help streamline the movement of goods from Point A to Point B. Federal officials also need to get tough on America's biggest economic rival, China, so that our country becomes less reliant on products from abroad.

REDUCING THE GOVERNMENT'S ROLE IN HEALTHCARE TO LOWER COSTS FOR SMALL BUSINESSES

Alma Beltran is a successful black entrepreneur, but she can't afford healthcare due to America's broken healthcare system. As the owner of Graphic Image Label in my childhood hometown of Chula Vista, California, Alma faces the tough choice between her business's health and her personal health—a dilemma that is all too common among minority entrepreneurs today.

"So far this year, I have not been able to afford paying my premium," explains Alma. "I must now decide between going without insurance and keeping my business, or closing my business so I can find a job with health coverage." Consider how this crushing dynamic depresses minority entrepreneurship nationwide.

Runaway healthcare costs have become one of the biggest barriers for small employers looking to hire and grow. According to the Kaiser Family Foundation, the average annual family healthcare premium at a small business with fewer than two hundred employees in 2022 was $22,186. Imagine how difficult it is for ordinary, low-margin small businesses to cover this outrageous cost while remaining profitable.

According to a 2021 survey by Small Business Majority, more than one in three small business owners say it's difficult to afford healthcare coverage, and more than two-thirds say the problem is getting worse. This challenge is especially difficult for minorities, whose businesses tend to have lower profit margins. Among black, Asian, and Latino respondents, 50 percent, 44 percent, and 43 percent, respectively, say that attaining health coverage is a challenge. Healthcare reform to lower prices would help many Americans and minority entrepreneurs most of all.

Entrepreneurs have been among the biggest victims of Obamacare. To acquire healthcare coverage, they are generally relegated to plans in the individual and small group markets that have both seen some of the biggest premium increases over the past several years.

Such plans are subject to numerous inflationary restrictions, including mandatory essential health benefits, that large employer group plans are not. This healthcare coverage disparity is just another example of how the deck is stacked against small businesses.

Mandatory essential health benefits, such as maternity and newborn care, mental health and substance abuse, and pediatric services, don't make sense for many small businesses. Yet these necessary additions dramatically drive up plan costs, putting a damper on funds that could otherwise be reinvested in the business. As a result of these skyrocketing healthcare costs, the number of small businesses offering health coverage fell by nearly one-third between 2008 and 2017.

HEALTHCARE FOR YOU INCREASES HEALTHCARE CHOICES WHILE REDUCING COSTS

JCN developed a pro-small business healthcare alternative called Healthcare for You—healthcare reform centered on the doctor-patient relationship and focused on clearing the bureaucrats and politicians from the exam room. Such healthcare reform empowers patients with choice and transparency, allowing small businesses to dramatically cut their healthcare costs if implemented.

Instead of relying on the government, which only drives up healthcare costs, Healthcare for You harnesses the market forces of choice, competition, and transparency to drive costs down. In contrast to government policies, market solutions eliminate backroom deals and hidden contracts that artificially inflate prices.

Healthcare for You would expand tax-free healthcare savings accounts, nontaxable portable insurance plans, and direct care at independent, price-transparent medical providers. These reforms would dramatically lower healthcare costs for entrepreneurs and small businesses.

These healthcare policy improvements would also allow Americans to be less tied to their employment healthcare coverage, allowing them to stay covered as they move between jobs and in and out of the labor market. Such reform would spur minority entrepreneurship in particular, as countless entrepreneurial minority employees would no longer remain stuck in dead-end jobs merely for the health benefits.

Eliminating and reducing regulations on physician paperwork, mandated essential benefits, and geographic and provider network limits would also significantly lower healthcare costs, allowing all

Americans to access coverage and care at lower prices.

Furthermore, the government can also help small businesses by allowing greater use of association health plans. AHPs empower small businesses to band together to purchase health insurance in bulk, lowering prices and mitigating risk. AHPs are also exempt from many of the burdensome regulations in Obamacare plans that drive up prices for entrepreneurs.

The Trump administration issued a rule in 2018 to expand AHPs to sole proprietors and ease requirements for them to be set up, yet a federal judge struck down the rule in 2019, leaving AHPs stuck in regulatory uncertainty.

The publication *Black Freelance* indicates the significant entrepreneurship dividends that cheaper healthcare options would have for minority sole-proprietorships:

> One of the most expensive and intimidating responsibilities that freelancers take on is health insurance. I talk to plenty of aspiring freelancers who're terrified of making *The Jump* because of the cost of insurance. And you know what? They have every reason to be concerned. Missing an insurance payment might not mean you're homeless or something's getting repossessed, but it can mean life-threatening and finance-destroying catastrophe if you have an accident or a health issue at the wrong time.

When combined with expanded tax-free health savings accounts that facilitate direct care at transparent, low prices, AHPs can make healthcare affordable again. These reforms will stop healthcare costs from being a hurdle to small business creation, especially minority small business creation. Instead, they will allow minority entrepreneurs like Alma to simultaneously protect their personal health and business health.

GREAT OPPORTUNITY PROJECT CAN IDENTIFY THE BEST STATE POLICIES TO BOOST MINORITY ENTREPRENEURS AND CLOSE RACIAL ECONOMIC GAPS

Supreme Court Justice Louis Brandeis called American states "the laboratories of democracy." Nowhere is this clearer than when it comes to identifying the best free-market policies to boost minority entrepreneurship. The most effective minority entrepreneurship public policies will filter up from the states, not be imposed by the federal government. JCN calls this effort to identify good public policy at the state level the Great Opportunity Project.

Consider the thirteen states that cut income taxes in 2021, helping residents and small businesses combat inflation costs and improve their economic situation. In Arizona, Governor Doug Ducey cut the state's income tax rate of 8 percent and 4.5 percent, depending on earnings, to a flat 2.5 percent—the lowest rate among states with an income tax.

This tax cut will accelerate Arizona's booming economy and keep it as a beacon for refugees fleeing California, whose top tax rate is 13.3 percent with a rate of nearly 10 percent for the middle class.

In Iowa, legislators and Governor Kim Reynolds created a flat tax and reduced the top tax rate on individuals from 8.5 percent to 3.9 percent while also reducing the corporate tax rate from 9.8 percent to 5.5 percent, eliminating a major barrier to entrepreneurs.

Similarly, Mississippi Governor Tate Reeves signed into law major tax reform, which has been spearheaded by Speaker of the House Philip Gunn for several years, reducing tax burdens and phasing in a 4 percent flat tax on personal income.

Governors Kevin Stitt (OK) and Brad Little (ID) both reduced personal and corporate income taxes last year, helping spur growth in their states. North Carolina also passed substantial income tax cuts in 2021, cutting its flat 5.25 percent personal income tax to 3.99 percent and implementing a complete phaseout of the corporate income tax. As the tax cut benefits to minority entrepreneurs in these states become obvious, other states will want to copy them to enjoy similar success.

States such as these that have passed free-market reforms to get the government out of the way of minority entrepreneurs have recovered from the pandemic far faster than big government states that have used the Covid-19 pandemic to further entrench their power. In contrast, states like California, Connecticut, Illinois, and New York have left small businesses on the hook to pay far higher unemployment insurance taxes in the years ahead. These Covid-era taxes burden employers at the worst possible time as they are forced to contend with numerous economic headwinds.

Similarly, major cities in these big government states have completed a disastrous experiment with "woke" district attorneys. They have fostered significant crime waves that disproportionately hurt minority small businesses, as they are more likely to be located in high-crime areas. Crime has led to a business exodus away from these cities and states, many of which haven't been able to regain their pre-pandemic workforces a full three years after the emergence of Covid-19.

States that have made the difficult decision to curtail welfare payments have also reaped economic rewards. Governors Greg Gianforte (MT) and Henry McMaster (SC) deserve special recognition for being the first two governors in the country to end enhanced federal unemployment benefits in June 2021. These governors faced withering media and political scrutiny for their actions, but their states' economies have greatly benefitted from accelerated job creation due to their leadership.

Texas and Florida have recently deregulated occupational licensing, making it easier for ordinary residents to ply their trades and start small businesses without paying thousands of dollars for unneeded certifications and trainings. As discussed in the last chapter, minorities are the biggest victims of these licenses.

Arizona, Arkansas, Florida, Georgia, Indiana, Iowa, Kansas, Maryland, Montana, New Hampshire, Oklahoma, and South Dakota all recently started or expanded their charter school programs, providing families with a lifeline to escape failing neighborhood schools. West Virginia also took a large step in reforming its education system when State Senator Patricia Rucker passed the Hope Scholarship, creating fully funded education savings accounts for nearly all state students.

Arizona, too, deserves credit for creating the nation's first universal education savings account program. It provides 1.1 million students in the state who choose to opt out of the neighborhood public school system with $7,000 to spend on a school of their choice, whether it's a charter school, Catholic school, or home school.

These educational choice reforms will help improve America's failing education system in which minorities are the biggest victims. Under the status quo, only about one in six black students in America are proficient in math or reading. Providing escape hatches from failing public schools will allow minorities to acquire the skills they need to succeed in entrepreneurship as young adults.

WELL-INTENDED GOVERNMENT POLICY OFTEN HAS UNINTENDED CONSEQUENCES THAT HURT MINORITY ENTREPRENEURS

Government policy is usually well-intended, but that sentiment is cold comfort to minority entrepreneurs stuck paying for the ensuing unintended consequences. This phenomenon is perhaps best evidenced by the consequences of Democrats' efforts—at both the legislative and executive levels of government—to enact a "joint-employer" standard on franchises and contractors.

Arcane labor law distinctions rarely make it to the top of the news cycle, but if enacted, such policy would absolutely devastate the minority entrepreneurship climate.

As the name implies, this standard would make franchisees and subcontractors joint employers with their franchisors or contractors. Proponents claim this relationship is necessary to make it easier to unionize vast swaths of the economy, such as the hotel and fast-food industries, ostensibly to generate better wages and working conditions for employees.

However, such a standard would disproportionately destroy minority franchisees who would lose their independence and need to report to their franchisors on all employment matters. Franchisors would become jointly liable for their franchisees' daily employment decisions.

To ward off potential lawsuits as joint employers, franchisors would have to curtail franchise opportunities, limiting them to the most qualified applicants and reducing business opportunities for minorities who often have to work harder for the same credentials. Minority-owned franchisees tend to operate in minority-owned neighborhoods and hire minority workers, meaning this standard also would reduce minority job opportunities.

One of the loudest voices against the implementation of this labor policy change is the Asian American Hotel Owners Association (AAHOA), whose mostly Indian American members own approximately half of the hotels in the nation. The AAHOA explains:

> What's the big problem with a nebulous joint-employer definition? It threatens to destroy the franchising and contracting business models upon which the economy is supported. These business models have also been proven routes to small business success for thousands of hoteliers and countless minority business owners.

Joint employer means joint liability. Under the joint-employer standard, franchisors and contractors could be responsible for the hundreds of daily decisions made by their franchisees and subcontractors. If a hotel's landscaping contractor screws up, the hotel could be sued.

To protect themselves from a slew of lawsuits, franchisors and contractors will have to become far more discerning in whom they franchise and contract. Established players with a long history of success: in. Risky upstarts trying to achieve the American Dream of small business ownership: out.

As a result, a joint employer standard will be a shot across the bow of the franchise and contracting business models. The franchise model alone is responsible for 13.3 million jobs and $1.6 trillion of GDP.

On almost every public policy issue, from spending to taxes to healthcare to labor policy, the best way the government can help small businesses, especially minority small businesses, is to simply do less. It's already difficult enough for minority entrepreneurs to find a product that fills a gap in the market and outcompete established players without simultaneously worrying about the government hamstringing them through bad policies.

With fewer government hurdles, minority entrepreneurs can more readily overcome racial economic gaps through their own inspiration and ingenuity.

CHAPTER 6: TIME TO REMEMBER THE FORGOTTEN SMALL BUSINESSMAN

In his legendary 1964 "A Time for Choosing" speech, President Ronald Reagan relayed the following anecdote:

> Not too long ago, two friends of mine were talking to a Cuban refugee, a businessman who had escaped from Castro, and in the midst of his story one of my friends turned to the other and said, "We don't know how lucky we are." And the Cuban stopped and said, "How lucky you are? I had someplace to escape to." And in that sentence he told us the entire story. If we lose freedom here, there's no place to escape to. This is the last stand on earth.

Nearly all Americans are descendants of those who came to this country to pursue a better life. In past generations, many who arrived—from the Irish, Italians, and Eastern Europeans to the Jews and even Catholics—were considered non-white minorities. The American free-market economy allowed these ethnic new arrivals the opportunity to ascend from poverty to relative wealth and close the "racial" wealth gaps among these groups.

The American entrepreneurship advantage can now generate the same wealth creation for the visible minorities who have arrived in America in recent generations. As I've demonstrated and explained in previous chapters, it already is! Minority entrepreneurship is closing racial economic wealth gaps as we speak. Yes, racial income and wealth divides persist, but greater entrepreneurship offers the best chance of closing them.

Unfortunately, big government policies, including reckless spending, tax increases, and countless regulations, threaten America's economic engine that has long overcome racial inequality. Ordinary Americans must redouble our efforts to protect the ladder of economic success. If America falls, there will be nowhere else for minorities to turn to better their economic station.

The United States still has an unparalleled minority entrepreneurship advantage. However, progressives and activists threaten to destroy it. If we let this occur, minorities will be hurt most of all, because they are often the most economically vulnerable to new costs associated with taxes, regulations, and inflation. The best pathway to reducing minority entrepreneurship economic gaps will be destroyed, and racial economic inequality will grow.

We don't know how lucky we are. Collectivists and leftists use Americans' general ignorance about our well-being to their advantage. If we realized how vulnerable our economy and standards of living really are, we wouldn't accept so many big government attacks on them.

America's vibrant entrepreneurship economy, the unique environment that provides unprecedented opportunity for minorities, is not fixed in nature like Lake Michigan or the Cascade Mountains. It results from free markets, individual rights, and limited government. To the extent that these prerequisites are destroyed by bad public policy, entrepreneurship opportunities will vanish.

AMERICANS FACE ANOTHER TIME FOR CHOOSING, EITHER FOR OR AGAINST ENTREPRENEURS

Americans now face another time for choosing. The country can either continue its "death by a thousand cuts" approach to small businesses—a path that disproportionately hurts minority entrepreneurs who generally have less capital, less education, and fewer connections—or it can double down on keeping the entrepreneurial ecosystem free from obstacles and putting small businesses ahead of, or at least alongside, every other interest group.

Unfortunately, we seem to be heading in the wrong direction. Observe the massive tax-and-spend legislation passed by President Biden and congressional Democrats in August 2022. The misnamed Inflation Reduction Act will fuel the inflationary fire, crushing entrepreneurs in the process. It spends $433 billion on Democrats' climate and healthcare projects, including extending expanded Obamacare subsidies that will further inflate healthcare premiums.

It also increases taxes on businesses, including small businesses, by more than $500 billion. It adds a football stadium's worth of new IRS agents to overwhelm small businesses with audits. Entrepreneurs don't keep tax lawyers and accountants on staff like their big business competitors; as such, they will be forced to settle with the IRS even if they've done nothing wrong. These new costs will make it harder for small businesses to expand and increase supply to bring down prices.

The nonpartisan Joint Committee on Taxation finds that most of the revenue collected from the law's tax hikes will be paid by everyday Americans earning less than $400,000, all while corporations, responsible to their shareholders, are forced to pass along tax increases in the form of higher prices to maintain their profit margins. Minority entrepreneurs and their customers will be among the legislation's biggest victims.

Change in Federal Taxes by Income Group Due to the Inflation Reduction Act in 2031 (in trillions of dollars)

Ordinary Americans earning less than $400,000 a year will pay approximately two-thirds of the tax revenue raised by the IRA

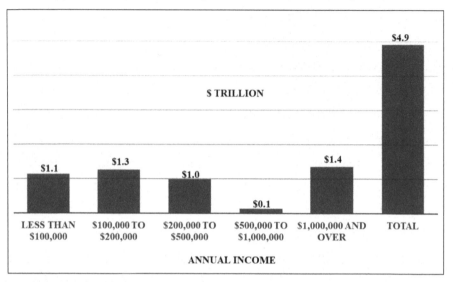

Source: Joint Committee on Taxation

This tax-and-spend legislation is just a taste of what's to come if big government activists increase their control of all three branches of government. If they succeed, it will mean the end of America's minority entrepreneurship advantage. Those from well-established and well-connected families will be far less affected by the ensuing entrepreneurship consequences than minorities, who tend to have fewer family connections and financial capital.

What's needed to reverse course? To start, a new recognition and celebration of forgotten small businesses. Every single new regulation or new piece of legislation should be viewed through the matrix of how it will affect small businesses. My organization is pushing to beef up the Small Business Regulatory Enforcement Fairness Act (SBREFA) of 1996, a federal statute forcing some federal agencies to consider the small business implications of their regulations. Any law or regulation that negatively impacts small businesses should not take effect, just as any housing development or public works project that violates the Endangered Species Act cannot currently be built.

But such political solutions are downstream from culture. Ultimately, what's needed to help preserve the minority entrepreneurship ecosystem is a renewed cultural appreciation for small businesses and their valuable role in society.

I'm not talking here of the banal, milquetoast support for small businesses that major companies regularly offer while simultaneously supporting every proposed big government regulation and tax increase. This entrepreneurship-washing is merely an attempt to generate positive PR by trading on the good name of small businesses.

Rather, what's needed is a fervent, automatic defense of small businesses akin to that given to teachers, pastors, sports teams, and other pillars of society. Such unconditional support will make it easier for minority entrepreneurs to fulfill their business and financial dreams.

TODAY'S FORGOTTEN MEN AND WOMEN ARE INCREASINGLY MINORITY ENTREPRENEURS

The 1883 essay "The Forgotten Man" by nineteenth-century American essayist and professor William Graham Sumner reads as if it were written yesterday. Sumner's essay celebrates the contributions made by ordinary workers, pointing out how popular social causes usurp these Americans' societal contributions.

Sumner explains the sociopolitical dynamic that treats such hardworking Americans as cows to be milked by governments:

> As soon as A observes something which seems to him to be wrong, from which X is suffering, A talks it over with B, and A and B then propose to get a law passed to remedy the evil and help X. Their law always proposes to determine what C

shall do for X ... I call [C] the Forgotten Man ... He is the man who never is thought of. He is the victim of the reformer, social speculator and philanthropist, and ... he deserves your notice both for his character and for the many burdens which are laid upon him.

See if Sumner's broader description of the Forgotten Man sounds familiar:

Who is the Forgotten Man? He is the simple, honest laborer, ready to earn his living by productive work. We pass him by because he is independent, self-supporting, and asks no favors. He does not appeal to the emotions or excite the sentiments. He only wants to make a contract and fulfill it, with respect on both sides and favor on neither side. ... We do not remember him because he makes no clamor ...

The Forgotten Man is delving away in patient industry, supporting his family, paying his taxes, casting his vote, supporting the church and the school, reading his newspaper, and cheering for the politician of his admiration, but he is the only one for whom there is no provision in the great scramble and the big divide.

Such is the Forgotten Man. He works, he votes, generally he prays—but he always pays—yes, above all, he pays. He does not want an office; his name never gets into the newspaper except when he gets married or dies. He keeps production going on. He contributes to the strength of parties. He is flattered before election. He is strongly patriotic. He is wanted, whenever, in his little circle, there is work to be done or counsel to be given. He may grumble some occasionally to his wife and family, but he does not frequent the grocery or talk politics at the tavern. Consequently, he is forgotten.

He is a commonplace man. He gives no trouble. He excites no admiration. He is not in any way a hero (like a popular orator); nor a problem (like tramps and outcasts); nor notorious (like criminals); nor an object of sentiment (like the poor and weak); nor a burden (like paupers and loafers); nor an object out of which social capital may be made (like the beneficiaries of church and state charities); nor an object for charitable aid and protection (like animals treated with cruelty); nor the object of a job (like the ignorant and illiterate); nor one over whom sentimental economists and statesmen can parade their fine sentiments (like inefficient workmen and shiftless artisans).

Therefore, he is forgotten. All the burdens fall on him, or on her, for it is time to remember that the Forgotten Man is not seldom a woman.

Is there any doubt that today's forgotten men and women are average entrepreneurs and small business owners? Reread the above excerpt and consider how well it applies to American small businesses toiling in today's economy that progressives consider theirs to control. I'd add one thing to Sumner's final sentence: it is also time to remember that the Forgotten Man and Woman are increasingly minorities.

PRESERVING MINORITY ENTREPRENEURSHIP PATHWAYS MEANS REMEMBERING THESE FORGOTTEN MEN AND WOMEN

To preserve the American entrepreneurship ecosystem that has allowed so many minorities to close the racial wealth gap, we must choose to remember these forgotten men and women. Sumner explains why it is so important to prioritize them over the latest social causes:

It is plain enough that the Forgotten Man and the Forgotten Woman are the very life and substance of society. They are the ones who ought to be first and always remembered. They are always forgotten by sentimentalists, philanthropists, reformers, enthusiasts, and every description of speculator in sociology, political economy, or political science ...

The Forgotten Man is weighted down with the cost and burden of the schemes for making everybody happy, with the cost of public beneficence, with the support of all the loafers, with the loss of all the economic quackery, with the cost of all the jobs. Let us remember him a little while. Let us take some of the burdens off him. Let us turn our pity on him instead of on the goodfornothing. It will be only justice to him, and society will greatly gain by it.

Why should we not also have the satisfaction of thinking and caring for a little about the clean, honest, industrious, independent, self-supporting men and women who have not inherited much to make life luxurious for them, but who are doing what they can to get on in the world without begging from anybody, especially since all they want is to be let alone, with good friendship and honest respect. Certainly the philanthropists and sentimentalists have kept our attention for a long time on the nasty, shiftless, criminal, whining, crawling, and good for nothing people, as if they alone deserved our attention. ...

I want to call to mind the Forgotten Man, because, in this case also, if we recall him and go to look for him, we shall find him patiently and perseveringly, manfully and independently struggling against adverse circumstances without complaining or begging. If, then, we are led to heed the groaning and complaining of others and to take measures for helping these others, we shall, before we know it, push down this man who is trying to help himself. ...

Wealth comes only from production, and all that the wrangling grabbers, loafers, and jobbers get to deal with comes from somebody's toil and sacrifice. Who, then, is he who provides it all? Go and find him and you will have once more before you the Forgotten Man. You will find him hard at work because he has a great many to support. Nature has done a great deal for him in giving him a fertile soil and an excellent climate and he wonders why it is that, after all, his scale of comfort is so moderate. He has to get out of the soil enough to pay all his taxes, and that means the cost of all the jobs and the fund for all the plunder.

We can either heed Sumner's words about the importance of the forgotten ordinary Americans toiling away at their small businesses, or we can continue treating them as a mere means to broader social ends. The latter approach will kill the geese that lay the nation's golden eggs and ultimately reverse our racial economic progress.

BIG GOVERNMENT PROPONENTS HAVE NO IDEA WHAT IT TAKES TO START A SMALL BUSINESS

Do any activists or progressives know how hard it is to actually start a small business? Do they appreciate the regulations, taxes, and hurdles involved, let alone the difficulty of providing a product or a service the market values? No, they don't. They have chosen to live off the production of small businesses rather than actually produce something the market values and the government allows.

In Ayn Rand's 1957 book *Atlas Shrugged*, businessmen and women stop "the motor of the world" by going on strike. They show the world what life would be like without the businesses they expropriate and take for granted. And it isn't pretty.

Today, we risk stopping the motor of the world by "laying off" entrepreneurs through big government actions that make it impossible for them to succeed. Minority entrepreneurs, who are always hit hardest by regulations, taxes, and inflation, would be the first to get pink slips. The potential consequences of following the big government choice in terms of economic vitality, living standards, and racial economic inequality would be grave.

DEFENDING SMALL BUSINESSES IS A CULTURAL AND INTELLECTUAL EXERCISE

How can we stand up for the forgotten men and women who run small businesses and defend their rights to improve their economic circumstances by trading value for value? We must commit to engaging with them culturally whenever and wherever we can. Our small businesses must be thought of as cultural, not mere economic, institutions.

Unfortunately, socialism is culturally ascendant. According to Gallup, 43 percent of Americans say socialism would be a good thing for the country. Increasing support for socialism—an economic system that relies on the government to redistribute property based on need and influence—is not surprising. Socialism has long received favorable treatment from cultural pillars such as the media, academia, Hollywood, and pop culture.

Additionally, millennials, now the country's largest generation, have been disproportionately hurt by recent higher education, healthcare, and housing cost increases. They blame these high costs on capitalism, though in actuality they are the products of government intervention in the economy.

Socialists take it as a given that capitalism creates racial inequality. Capitalists and small business proponents must fight this message with everything they have. Minority entrepreneurship success—the fact that minority entrepreneurs outearn whites—demonstrates that capitalism overcomes racial economic inequality rather than spreading it.

Keeping entrepreneurship pathways open through free markets and limited government, therefore, is the best way to achieve not only socialists' but everyone's racial equality aims.

While this pro-entrepreneurship effort requires relentless marketing and creative communications, it's ultimately an intellectual undertaking. In practice, this means explaining the logical flaws and internal contradictions of socialist positions wherever and whenever possible.

The vibrant and racially diverse American middle class, full of entrepreneurs, is the best argument against socialism. If capitalism creates inequality, this massive middle class shouldn't exist. If the class differences in America are so stark, how do we account for this historic middle class?

Where does the middle class truly not exist? The answer: in socialist countries, where there are just two groups—fabulously wealthy government apparatchiks, and the rest of the population, who are paupers. The United States, where nearly everyone has an iPhone and air conditioning and the opportunity to pursue entrepreneurship, is strikingly equal by comparison. Big government proponents have a vested interest in pretending the minority small business success story doesn't exist, because it is a testament to the wealth-creating power of capitalism.

One of the defining characteristics of capitalism is entrepreneurship, which capitalism fosters and socialism forbids. In America, citizens are free to start businesses of their choosing. In socialist countries, entrepreneurship is largely either explicitly or implicitly forbidden. Minorities are "stuck" in socialist countries but have immense income mobility in America.

Capitalism is the only system that creates wealth for everyone, even the poor. Socialism—"seizing the means of production"—merely redistributes the wealth around. As Margaret Thatcher noted, the problem with socialism is that "you eventually run out of other people's money." Now more than ever, Americans must hear this truth that capitalism creates and socialism takes.

Convincing Americans of the power of free markets and individual liberty can advance minority entrepreneurship. As Sumner explains:

What the Forgotten Man needs is that we come to a clearer understanding of liberty and to a more complete realization of it. Every step which we win in liberty will set the Forgotten Man free from some of his burdens and allow him to use his powers for himself and for the commonwealth.

STANDING UP FOR SMALL BUSINESSES IS NOT A HEARTLESS POSITION—IT'S THE BEST WAY TO HEAL AMERICA'S RACIAL DIVIDE

Almost every time government solutions are proposed, they are likely to come at the expense of small businesses. Activists may claim the taxes they need to fund their latest proposals only affect "the millionaires and billionaires," but treat this claim like the advance of a leper's bell. In truth, there are simply not enough rich people to fund their plans. They will also have to target entrepreneurs and the middle class for the same reason Willie Sutton robbed banks: because that's where the money is.

In fact, Sumner suggests that every time activists talk of helping "underserved populations," that is the time to rise immediately to the defense of forgotten small businesses:

> The warning to you to look for the Forgotten Man comes the minute that the orator or writer begins to talk about the poor man. That minute the Forgotten Man is in danger of a new assault, and if you intend to meddle in the matter at all, then is the minute for you to look about for him and to give him your aid … Hence you must be prepared to be told that you favor the capitalist class, the enemy of the poor man …

Sumner's point about being called heartless for defending small businesses is insightful. Americans support social causes that come at the expense of small businesses in a large part because they want to seem compassionate.

Yet, as I've explained in this book, there is no dichotomy between supporting small businesses and defending minorities and the poor. A vibrant free-market economy with limited government intervention is precisely what offers minorities the best opportunity to close racial economic divides. Supporting small businesses and supporting minorities go hand in hand. This is the truly compassionate approach. Be prepared to be told that you favor the capitalist class, but reject the notion that this support means you oppose minorities.

In fact, to the extent that big government initiatives hamstring the free market, progressives are the real enemy of minorities and the poor. Their good intentions stand in stark contrast to the bad outcomes their policies inflict upon minority entrepreneurs whose business dreams are often crushed as a result.

Take comfort in Sumner's words:

> I suppose that the first chemists seemed to be very hard-hearted and unpoetical persons when they scouted the glorious dream of the alchemists that there must be some process for turning base metals into gold. … Let us put down now the cold, hard fact and look at it just as it is. There is no device whatever to be invented for securing happiness without industry, economy, and virtue.

Small businesses, and increasingly minority-run small businesses, are the closest thing we have to alchemists in the world today, creating wealth and value where none existed before. Minority entrepreneurs forge middle-class lives and financial security from almost nothing. The alchemy performed by countless minority entrepreneurs such as Carlton Guthrie, Carlos Gazitua, Carlos Ruiz, and Dina Rubio demonstrates that minority entrepreneurship is the best way to overcome America's racial economic divides, form a more perfect union, and ensure domestic tranquility.

Minority entrepreneurs are the real revolutionaries—not the activists you read about in books and the media. Let's accelerate this race revolution by choosing to stand up for small businesses and telling the government to do less, not more.